W9-BRG-660

TECHNIQUES OF
STAINED GLASS

LEADED, FACETED, & LAMINATED GLASS

VINCENT O'BRIEN

 VAN NOSTRAND REINHOLD COMPANY
New York Cincinnati Toronto London Melbourne

ACKNOWLEDGMENTS

The author would like to thank the many individual stained glass craftsmen and studios who generously contributed photos of their work as well as supplying invaluable background information.

Many people supplied technical assistance which has been of great value to the scope of the work; my thanks to Mr. William L. Jamison, Technical Director, Thermoset Plastics, Inc., for his advice on faceted glass procedures; to Mr. William H. Kuenning, Associate Editor of *Concrete Construction* for guidance on the methods of concrete and glass; to Dr. Harvey Johnstone, dermatologist, for his counsel on safety precautions in the studio. My thanks also to the Stained Glass Association of America for their many and varied publications on the craft.

I am especially appreciative of the generous advice—as well as the warm encouragement given by my friends, author Lillian de la Torre Bueno, Professor Emeritus George S. McCue, and Dr. Tom Ross, Colorado College.

Printed in the United States of America
Designed by Loudan Enterprises

Published in 1977 by Van Nostrand Reinhold Company
A division of Litton Educational Publishing, Inc.
135 West 50th Street, New York, N.Y. 10020 U.S.A.

Van Nostrand Reinhold Limited
1410 Birchmount Road, Scarborough, Ontario M1P 2E7, Canada

Van Nostrand Reinhold Australia Pty. Limited
17 Queen Street, Mitcham, Victoria 3132, Australia

Van Nostrand Reinhold Company Limited
Molly Millars Lane, Wokingham, Berkshire, England

16 15 14 13 12 11 10 9 8 7 6 5 4 3 2

Library of Congress Cataloging in Publication Data

O'Brien, Vincent, 1919-
  Techniques of stained glass.

  Bibliography: p.
  Includes index.
  1. Glass craft. I. Title.
TT298.O27   748.5   77-77969
ISBN 0-442-26259-0

CONTENTS

AUTHOR'S NOTE

Not too many years ago, the only way to learn how to do stained glass work was to join the ranks of apprentices in gloomy back shops of stained glass studios. There, the secrets of the trade were judiciously guarded, as were the store of hundred-year-old designs, for they would probably serve tomorrow's needs.

Today, the picture has changed considerably and, generally speaking, much for the better; many universities and community schools, even some local parks and recreation departments, offer classes in stained glass. Many people, who may find it outside their budget, or inconvenient to take classes are taking up the craft on their own, turning the kitchen table, the basement, or the garage into their workshop. In fact, more than a few young professionals in stained glass have gotten started this way.

As a result, a considerable number of books have been published to answer the needs of this movement. However, many of the books written on techniques and studio practices concentrate almost totally on the mechanics and processes of the craft, all too often leaving the question of design and the encouragement of one's personal creativity entirely out of the picture. In fact, some books openly encourage the copying of archaic, ready-made patterns (from medieval to Victorian and even "modernistic"). This fosters a subtle implication that stained glass is just the thing for those with nimble fingers, a lot of patience, and not much imagination. Nothing could be farther from the truth; yet, be-cause of this, a disservice is being done to the many people who might otherwise have wanted to get involved with it either as a hobby or as a more serious study.

I have attempted in this book to encourage the idea of individual creativity in stained glass at whatever level—beginning or advanced—by emphasizing the free use of the imagination during the sketch or idea stage; the text is illustrated with examples of contemporary works in a variety of techniques that display innovative concepts as well as masterful technical control.

If stained glass is to continue to grow and flourish as a vital art form, which it has certainly begun to do in the past fifteen years, then it is especially important that beginners in stained glass be exposed to alternatives other than the outmoded, though still practiced, method of copying stock designs. One rationale behind this old approach is that it is a "safer" method that will be abandoned once more technical skill has been achieved. Actually, what this amounts to is the postponement of the opportunity to do something that is really your own. And it is also quite likely that once you start out with many of the decisions and choices already made for you, you will find it too ready a convenience to do without and will simply continue to depend upon it. The very act of choosing the colors of glass (whether bright or subtle), as well as the textures of glass (whether bold or plain), is the beginning of a selective process that is individual to you; then, the way in which you choose to combine the colors in a design is another small, but significant, step in making something that is your own work. The copying system, on the other hand, which is not far away from "stained glass by-the-numbers," almost precludes that you will ever turn out unique work.

Another purpose of this book (again, with the beginner in mind) is to explain and illustrate, in as clear and concise a manner as possible, the technical rudiments of leaded glass work, which are really not as complex nor as difficult as many people seem to believe. I hope the notion that one's mechanical ability is *the* vital factor will be dispelled once and for all.

Generally, most beginners in stained glass get their start in the leaded glass technique. On the other hand, many people have worked with leaded glass for years without being aware of the beautiful new possibilities presented by the more recent developments in the faceted glass and laminated glass techniques. Those with some previous experience in leaded glass will find that that particular chapter covers ground that is already familiar to them. The information on faceted glass and laminated glass, however, is considerably more comprehensive. It should serve as a solid base for those experienced glass workers who want to add these techniques to their repertoire of skills, preparing them to achieve and carry out commissions of a professional or commercial nature.

Because of the very diverse backgrounds, professions, and educations of people who are taking up the study of stained glass, the scope of the book is not directed to any specific level of experience. Some, for example, will bring extensive designing or drawing ability to the craft, while others may have studied no sort of art work at all. For these people, the joining of an art class or the reading of a book on art appreciation or on the basics of design would provide an excellent adjunct when beginning stained glass work. At any rate, there is a curious phenomenon that is peculiar to stained glass and may help to explain part of its *mystique* as an art form; the efforts of some beginners, which would probably look thoroughly hopeless if carried out in painting or in sculpture, will frequently take on considerable charm when done in stained glass—much to everyone's surprise.

This effect may be related to the fact that stained glass work need not be made up of a great number of pieces of glass to be a pleasant thing to look at; nevertheless, much stained glass work being done today reflects a compulsion to use a countless number of small glass pieces cut into complex shapes and in every color available. It all adds up to a style that might be called "Pizza-Gothic." This tendency is reinforced by a current indulgence in nostalgia for things past (whether they were ugly or not—no matter). This is not to say that the lovely works of Louis Comfort Tiffany, for example, should not be enjoyed for the beautiful things they were; but they cannot be *"recreated,"* and the entire practice of producing instant antiques is a very dubious one.

Finally, I have had in mind that this book would seem an appropriate place to set out some brief, but pertinent, professional guidelines—some cautions and encouragements for the increasing number of people who may be considering the prospect of starting an independent studio or stained glass business.

BACKGROUND

That we are in the midst of a new wave of interest and creativity in the art of stained glass (perhaps it is not too early to say renaissance) is amply evident.

Stained glass techniques had remained virtually unchanged from the early Gothic period until well into the twentieth century. Traditionally, stained glass has consisted of a design of various colors of glass that have been cut, painted, and fired, and which are then assembled into a pattern held together by a matrix of strips of lead, called "cames."

In our time we have seen the development of beautiful, new stained glass techniques, such as "faceted" slab glass and laminated glass, as well as bold experimentation with stained glass in sculpture. In what had only recently been called a lost art, we now find a vital art form, not only alive and kicking, but dancing as well.

It was not until the twentieth century that something new under the sun in the art of stained glass began to emerge. Beginning in the 1930s, artists explored the use of thick glass (1 inch or more in thickness, as contrasted with about 1/8 inch used in traditional stained glass). From France, where these innovations began, came the term "dalles de verre," literally meaning flagstones of glass. It has come to be known in English-speaking countries as "dalles" or as "slab glass," and is also referred to as "faceted" glass, after the process of chipping the edges.

Since lead cames, traditionally used in stained glass work, would not suffice to hold the thick pieces of glass together, a mixture of concrete was used. This concrete matrix was further strength-ened with the addition of metal reinforcing rods running through the structure.

Largely as a result of research in the aircraft industry during World War II, high-strength adhesives, called epoxy adhesives, came into use. The unique qualities of the epoxy resins, with their high compressive, flexural, and tensile strengths (as well as their excellent coefficient of expansion and contraction) offered broad and interesting new possibilities to artists working in glass.

As an art form, stained glass has responded, though only recently, to the modern spirit of experimentation, improvisation, and individualistic creativity that is characteristic of our time. One fundamental change in the art is reflected in a social context—a gradual movement away from the "religious art" connotation that has been synonymous with stained glass from its earliest use. To be sure, the most widespread use of stained glass continues to be in ecclesiastical architecture, and it has reflected many changes in response to the new aesthetics of church design. However, stained glass is increasingly becoming accepted for its purely artistic merits in civic and commercial buildings. In addition to its development as an architectural art, it has burgeoned into a variety of decorative craftwork and also into its most recent form—as an independent, personal art statement.

One of the unique qualities of faceted slab glass is the physical attractiveness of the material itself. The inch-thick glass pieces have a strong and rugged character; yet, the faceting, or chipping, of the edges gives them a gemlike, delicate sparkle. The various colors of the glass not only transmit light, but seem to entrap and *engage* it in a luminous action. In skillfully done slab glass work, the quality of the color can have a depth, a clarity, and a vibrance that is quite unmatched in any other art form. Its appeal seems to be immediate, sensual, and emotional, rather than cerebral or intellectual.

The first time I saw an example of faceted slab glass work was some twenty-three years ago when I was an art student in France. I was more than intrigued by it. To use that banal, but very descriptive phrase, it was a case of love at first sight. I wanted to get my hands into this attractive medium as soon as possible. But getting started proved a little discouraging at first. It seemed that the libraries, the glass industry, and the technical publications would yield only scant bits of information at a time concerning these innovations in an ancient craft. The technique of slab glass, which was such a complete departure from the time-honored traditions of leaded, painted, and fired glass, was so recent a development as an art form that nothing comprehensive had been published.

In the intervening years a variety of books, pamphlets from industries, and publications of the Stained Glass Association of America have given us many additional reference guides. This knowledge, however, is fragmented into a bewildering number of diverse sources, so today's artists and craftsmen may find it both time-consuming and not a little confusing to bring the various theories and procedures together. One would find, for example, a chapter on faceted glass in a book mainly devoted to leaded, stained glass; an article on laminated glass would be buried in a volume that concentrated on fiberglass and Styrofoam construction; yet another chapter on glass in concrete would be found in a trade publication mainly concerned with concrete engineering.

The aim of this book is to present a concise focus on the three main types of stained glass work; an overview of the leaded glass method is given, while procedures for faceted glass, as well as for laminated glass, are presented in more complete detail.

Listing specific costs for the various tools and supplies that will be mentioned has been purposely avoided; current rapid changes in these costs might soon make the information misleading

Because of the very diverse and experimental nature of the techniques of painting, firing and fusing of glass, no attempt has been made to incorporate them here; several references for further reading in this area are given in the Appendix.

It is also beyond the scope of this book to present, other than in passing, the fascinating history of stained glass, the origins of which can be traced back to the early Egyptian dynasties. It need hardly be said that reading in this area will provide a sense of involvement and identification with this singular *métier*.

CHAPTER 1

THE WORK SPACE

While neatness may not be a great virtue in a studio, organization is. This is especially true when working with glass since the craft involves sequential, methodical, procedures; each step requires that its particular tool or material be on hand at the right time.

Naturally, the larger the work space you can afford, the better. Note, however, that the amount of room needed for leaded glass work is less than what is required for faceted glass. In any case, whether you will be using a corner of the garage or a vacant wing of your chateau, these things are desirable:

1. A sufficient amount of daylight so that glass colors can be properly perceived and work in progress judged against daylight.

2. A dependable space-heating system, not so much for comfort, but for maintaining proper curing temperatures, when necessary.

3. Adequate ventilation as a safety precaution against noxious fumes.

A large, flat table will be required, or, if you have the space, several of these. They can be of a simple arrangement of plywood sheets laid flat on sawhorses. Preferably, though, they should be of a more stable construction, with the ability to withstand rough usage, such as hammering; they should not easily be knocked off balance during the process of working.

An arrangement I like is to start with a very stoutly constructed table of about 3 by 6 feet (91 by 180 cm). (The height should be made according to whether you are tall or short; almost all the work at the table is done standing up.) This table can be built of used construction lumber; the use of 4- by 4-inch (10- by 10-cm) posts for the legs will give the table great solidity. On the rough surface of this table can be laid 3/4-inch (19-mm) plywood panels that are leveled up and held in place with a few nails. Aside from being very solid, the advantage of this kind of table is that you can take off the top plywood panel and store it should you need the space in your studio for some other project. Meanwhile, you have a rugged work table that can still be moved around but that will not use up much of your valuable space.

STORAGE SUGGESTIONS

Any type of strongly built bookshelf construction will suffice for storing the 8- by 12-inch (20- by 30-cm) slabs of glass that are used in faceted glass work. A convenient arrangement is to build the racks against the wall rather than have them jut out into the studio space. Be sure the shelves are well anchored into the wall since each slab weighs approximately 7 pounds (3.2 kg).

Used 2- by 8-inch (5- by 20-cm) planks and some bricks can make inexpensive and adaptable shelves, but they must be well attached to the wall. For lumber of smaller dimension, you will need more vertical supports to safely carry the weight of the slabs.

1-1. A convenient means of storing slab glass uses 2- by 8-inch construction lumber and bricks. Care must be taken to anchor the shelves firmly to the wall; each slab weighs approximately 7 pounds (3.10 kg).

Storage of the 1/8-inch (3-mm) colored glass used in the leaded and laminated glass processes is an equally simple matter. The sheets should be stored on edge in open racks, with enough space left so that you can easily reach in and slide them out for inspection. Covering these open-front racks with a cloth or some sort of simple curtain arrangement helps greatly to minimize dust accumulation on your glass (see drawing on page 46).

CHAPTER 2.

WORKING WITH FACETED GLASS

While the basic technique of leaded stained glass is founded on a centuries-old tradition, the more recently developed faceted glass process is not nearly so well known or as documented in detail. Just as the two techniques differ markedly, so does the visual character and *effect* of the finished work; we admire the delicacy and weblike beauty of leaded glass. In contrast, we are impressed with the rugged character of faceted glass, with the depth and glow of its color. The basic materials involved in the two processes reflect an equal contrast; leaded glass work consists of thin panes of glass that are held together with a filigree of lead strips, while faceted glass calls for the use of glass pieces that are about seven times thicker and that are bound together in a sturdy matrix of epoxy resin or concrete.

This chapter outlines the technique of faceted glass set in epoxy. (For the procedures of faceted glass set in concrete, see Chapter 3.) The procedures involved can be set out as follows:

1. Developing the design.
2. Making the cartoon.
3. Preparing the work surface.
4. Cutting and shaping the glass.
5. Faceting the glass.
6. Applying the mold release.
7. Mixing and pouring the epoxy resin.
8. Texturing the epoxy resin.
9. The curing process.
10. Finishing the panels.

(Safety precautions in handling epoxy and a table for calculating epoxy supply needs are also included in the chapter).

SLAB GLASS

The terms used to describe the thick slabs of glass need brief clarification. They have been called "dalles de verre" (from their French origin) or simply "slab glass." However, faceting—the chipping of the edges of the glass—is unique to this type of work and seems a more descriptive term as well. Thus, we will refer to the basic glass material as *slab glass* and to the finished work as *faceted glass*. In answer to the question, "Is faceted glass *stained glass*?" the answer is yes, in the sense that the color is integral throughout the depth of the glass slabs. In addition, the term "faceted stained glass" seems to have been accepted into fairly common usage.

Both American and European manufacturers of slab glass make the glass units in modules of 8 by 12 inches (20 by 30 cm). They generally average 7/8 inch thick, but may vary from 3/4 to 1 1/8 inches (1.9 cm to 2.9 cm). It is also possible to get 8- by 8-inch (20- by 20-cm) slabs and up to 2-inch-thick slabs (5 cm). (See Appendix for sources of supply.)

Manufacturers produce the slabs of various colors by pouring the molten glass into open molds.

2-1. An example of faceted glass work showing variations from very thin to very wide areas in the "black line" pattern. Our eye tends to perceive the light and color of the glass pieces as the "positive," or active, elements of the design, but the pattern and movement of the total composition is greatly influenced and supported by the "negative," or passive, matrix of the epoxy areas. Detail of the Chapel Window from the First Presbyterian Church, Bartlesville, Oklahoma. Designed and executed by Willet Studio. (Photo by Willet Studio)

The different colors are obtained by adding mineral oxides while the molten glass is still in the crucibles. The molds then move through an annealing oven, where they are allowed to cool very gradually. This carefully controlled cooling process is necessary so that the glass will achieve the proper temper, or internal tension—that is, not too brittle—enabling it to be cut easily and preventing it from shattering when it is faceted. The bottom of the mold leaves a coarsely textured imprint on the slab, while the top area, which is exposed to the air, is very smooth and shiny. Entrapped bubbles, as well as small craterlike extrusions on the surface, add to the interesting texture of slab glass panels.

Slab glass is expensive and, depending on your location, it is sometimes difficult to find a convenient source of supply. The question inevitably arises: "What about making my own glass slabs?" Some artists do, but they are very few in number—and for very good reason. To successfully make slab glass is a tricky bit; it requires technical knowledge best learned from someone who has had an extensive background in the process. Doing it on your own is possible, but will definitely require a much larger investment of time. Also, considerably more working space will be required—not to mention the necessary outlay of money for equipment and supplies. In short, making your own glass, either slabs or flat-colored sheets, is definitely not recommended for anyone in the beginning stages of glass work.

If your first project in faceted glass is to be a modest one—just to get acquainted with the particular feeling of the medium—it is best to buy some "remnants" and miscellaneous broken pieces of slab glass from the nearest stained glass studio that works with slab glass. (Most larger cities have a number of commercial studios that will sell remnants. Otherwise, you can order it by mail. See Appendix for supply sources.) Various pieces of these odd-shaped remnants can be arranged into a design for a small panel. However, if the spirit moves you to a more ambitious and serious approach, your first work in faceted glass will be more involved with the important experience of *designing* and then shaping the glass to fit your design. At the same time, this need not require more than several slabs of a few colors. In any event, the procedure remains the same.

TOOLS

The tools needed for faceted glass work are fewer and simpler than those required for leaded glass. Also, the skills required are less demanding in terms of finesse or refinement of detail.

Chisel. The most challenging part of working with slab glass is the cutting. For this you will need a long chisel. This tool cannot be bought but is easily made from a short section of T beam, as shown in the illustration. Your local welding shop should have no difficulty in making this tool to your order. The dimensions are not critical, although the stem of the T beam should be at least 3 inches (7.6 cm) high. The cutting edge of this long chisel should be ground evenly, but should not be extremely sharp, since it would be dulled quickly in use and would tend to wear unevenly. Though not essential, there is an advantage to having a bead of some hard metal, such as tungsten, put along the cutting edge; this type of edge will take much more wear than will a mild steel edge. This chisel should be mounted solidly with screws into a section of wood log or other heavy block of wood. A final consideration is to set the chisel on a box or sturdy platform so that it is at a comfortable working height of approximately 30 inches (76 cm). This type of homemade chisel is the most basic tool in faceted glass work; with it you will be able to break the slabs along straight line cuts.

2-3a. The glass is first scored with a glass cutter; then the score is positioned over the chisel.

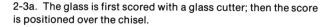

2-3b. The glass is brought smartly down on the chisel, the hands helping to snap the glass apart.

BEAD OF HARD METAL ON TIP

"T" BEAM WITH FLANGE REMOVED

HOLES FOR MOUNTING IN WOOD BASE

2-2. A long chisel made from a "T" beam.

Hardy. After it has been broken to size on the long chisel, you will need another form of chisel, called a *"hardy,"* to *shape* the glass. (The term comes from the blacksmith trade; it is sometimes called a "fuller" and sometimes, mistakenly, an "anvil".) Finding one of these might be difficult since blacksmithing is not so widely practiced as it once was. If necessary, this tool can be made at a welding shop. Its general shape is shown in the illustration; the cutting edge, approximately 2 inches (5 cm) long, should be beaded with a hard metal that occasionally can be sharpened. There is an advantage to mounting the base of the hardy securely into a sturdy wood block. It gives a very solid support when you break glass over it; yet, when necessary, you can still pry the hardy out of its support.

A smaller hardy can be made by having a cold chisel welded to a metal base which can be securely fastened into a wood base.

Glass Cutter. A glass cutter, the same type as used in leaded glass work, will be needed to score the glass slabs before breaking them on the chisel.

2-4. Shaping of slab glass pieces is done with a chipping hammer and a "hardy" chisel, which is firmly mounted in a wood stump.

Chipping Hammer. For the shaping of each piece of glass in your design, as well as for the faceting or chipping of the edges, you will need a chipping hammer. Some artists use only one; some prefer several of different weights. A mason's or tilesetter's hammer, available at hardware stores, can be used for breaking the smaller pieces of slab glass.

A more heavy-duty type of chipping hammer, which may not be so available as a mason's hammer, consists of a bulky, two-edged piece of hard steel with a short wooden handle; the heavy weight of the head does much of the work. A helpful device is a cone of rubber (made from an automobile inner-tube), which is put over the handle in the manner of a handguard on a sword; this will protect your hands from any flying fragments of glass.

Lapidary Saw. Another tool which is extremely useful for working in slab glass is a lapidary saw. With this saw, you can slice through thick slabs of glass in much the same way as you would cut lumber on a table saw. While it requires a fair investment of money, for one who is intent on carrying out architectural or commercial commissions, it is well worth the cost. It is worth noting, however, that equipment such as the lapidary saw is by no means a necessity; I have seen exquisite work produced with the basic tools already described.

This type of saw is used extensively in lapidary work and is available in most parts of the country. (For supply sources see Appendix.) The lapidary saw is designed for cutting rocks and semiprecious stones, but it is readily adaptable for cutting glass. It consists of a circular blade (preferably the 10-inch-diameter blade), the edge of which is tipped with a myriad of tiny industrial diamonds.

For most lapidary work the blade is run in a lubricating bath of light cutting-oil. However, glass being a fairly soft material in the scale of minerals, the blade can safely be run in water. While the blade may not last quite as long this way, it is really a minor consideration in view of the advantages; the oil vaporizes into the air and, unless bothersome precautions are taken, you will be breathing this unhealthy stuff. In addition, it would be disastrous to get oil on your glass since the epoxy will not adhere to it. Another advantage of operating the blade in water is that the tool can be well sluiced out from time to time. This will prevent a build-up of the finely powdered glass sludge that is produced in the process of cutting.

The lapidary saw is extremely useful where long, thin shapes of glass are needed to be formed. Actually, it is impossible to achieve these without the lapidary saw no matter how skillful you may be with the chipping hammer. Also, mortising, cutting acute angles, and making such demanding shapes as letters are much easier to do with the saw than with the chipping hammer. Last, but not least, is the fact that there is considerably less wastage of glass when the lapidary saw is used; there is no question that in time the lapidary saw will pay for itself in glass saved.

The diamond-tipped blade of the lapidary saw is quite safe to use. In contrast to the ripping action of most lumber-cutting blades, the cutting edge of the lapidary blade is quite smooth; it performs its cutting with a gradual abrasive force. The glass is pushed slowly against the blade. The width of the cut is about 1/16 inch (approximately 1.5 mm).

It is advisable to wear rubber gloves and a face mask when working with the lapidary saw, since very small splinters are sometimes produced in the cutting process. Another note of precaution when using the lapidary saw: Since it is powered by electricity, it is very important to ensure that the motor is properly grounded and that the motor, the switch, and the wiring are completely "isolated" from the water supply. Use plastic shields, waterproof tape, or similar precautions. In short, see to it that even if some water is accidentally splashed on the apparatus, the electrical elements will remain completely dry and safe.

Miscellaneous Tools. Needless to say, you should always wear a face mask when breaking or faceting the slabs of glass. Goggles, which protect only the eye area, are not nearly so safe as a face mask. Also, wearing the protective goggles over spectacles can be bothersome.

Aside from an assortment of smaller items, such as spatulas, brushes, and so forth, the basic tools for working in slab glass do not involve much expense. There are other types of studio equipment that will be mentioned later, but while they may be very helpful, they are not absolutely necessary.

2-5. The lapidary saw, with its diamond-tipped blade running in water, is well adapted to cutting a variety of different shapes in slab glass.

MATERIALS

Unlike leaded glass, faceted glass work involves a *casting* process; it utilizes a material that changes from a flowing state to a solid state to hold the whole assemblage of glass pieces together. Either epoxy resins or concrete (see Chapter 3) can be used for this purpose. A liquid mold release is also used as an aid in the casting process. The following is a description of these materials in the order of their use.

Mold Release. Before pouring the epoxy resin, a mold release must be used. The release agent should do two jobs: It should prevent the wood frame of the mold, as well as the transparent parting sheet, from coming in contact with the epoxy resin. Secondly, it should prevent the poured epoxy from seeping underneath the various pieces of glass in your design.

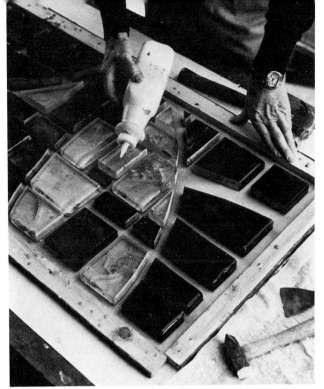

2-8. Used as a mold release, liquid latex is poured between the glass pieces from a plastic bottle with a small spout. The latex must cure overnight before epoxy is poured.

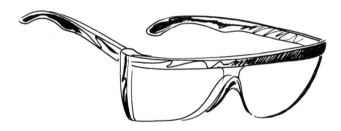

2-6. Safety goggles protect only the eye area.

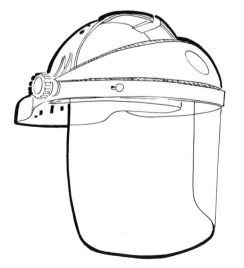

2-7. The shield face mask provides maximum safety when working with glass.

Liquid latex, a synthetic rubberlike substance, is ideally suited for this purpose. In addition, it has other useful applications in sculpture and general studio practice. Other types of release agents made with oil or grease bases are not only messy to work with, but could seriously interfere with the bond between glass and epoxy; by all means, avoid them.

Epoxy Resin. As used in faceted glass work, epoxy resins are very "compatible" with glass; that is, they have a favorable coefficient of expansion and contraction in relation to that of glass. This is very important in terms of the structural integrity of the finished panels, since glass is highly affected by temperature changes and reacts to them by expanding and contracting. It must be remembered, too, that a darker color of glass will absorb much more solar heat than its lighter neighbor; thus, the cast matrix of faceted glass must be able to accommodate, without cracking, the uneven tensions that result. Another good point about epoxy resin is that, due to its very high strength, it does not require reinforcement.

15

Epoxy resins are expensive materials, but for the results obtained, the ease in handling, and, above all, the unusual physical properties of its compressive, tensile, and flexural strengths, there is nothing quite like them. You will find that there are many epoxy formulations on the market; they are being used for everything from sealing roofs to patching airplanes. However, it is advisable to buy only the epoxy that has been specially formulated for use in slab glass work and to get it from a manufacturer that has been established for some time. The type of epoxy resin used in faceted glass is an industrial product; that is, it is not generally available to the public through the usual hardware outlets. (See Appendix for sources of supply.)

The epoxy resins are available in a range of colors, from white to neutral browns, grays, and charcoal. You can also mix your own color with the addition of earth colors or mortar black. These are in powder form and are readily available in most hardware or paint stores. Remember, too, that if you want to scatter sand or other materials over the epoxy surface before it has set up, the color of that material will dominate whatever color the epoxy may be. When a faceted glass panel has been completed and set in a wall so that light comes through the glass, even if the color of the epoxy is light or even white, the epoxy matrix inevitably appears as a black line between the colors. This is a curious and not always self-evident effect.

DEVELOPING THE DESIGN

One of the interesting characteristics of faceted glass is that the "black line" separating the colors becomes an important and *active,* rather than passive, part of the total effect; it can be a very thin line or it can be sufficiently wide to function as an area of black space. In contrast, the black line in leaded work is generally made up of lead lines of a constant width. Sometimes several widths are combined in one panel; but, generally speaking, the effect of the black line in leaded glass is of a "neutral" nature in the sense that it is confined to separating one color area from another. If the leaded glass work is painted and fired, then the rigidity, or gridlike effect, is vastly ameliorated; in masterful work, the black line fuses harmoniously into the overall design. These days, however, much work is being done in leaded glass that is not painted; a greater emphasis is placed on the "pure" quality of natural glass and, consequently, the lead lines play a more prominent role in the design.

Faceted glass is generally not painted and fired, though some have experimented in this direction. It relies more upon a feeling of massiveness and strength, rather than delicacy, while the faceting suggests a depth and liveliness of active, rather than muted, color.

There is another interesting optical effect in faceted glass. The greater the black area intervals between colors, the more intense and deeper the colors appear to be. In the hands of an experienced artist this can result in a very vivid graphic effect. Much seems to depend on the *variations* of black intervals; without sufficient dynamic contrasts (thick versus thin elements and straight versus curved elements) in the black line pattern of the design, rather static effects of isolated islands of color that do not *interact* with one another are obtained.

There is probably no "best way" to start your designs for faceted glass, but the most direct method is to draw it, full-size, directly on a large piece of paper.

Another method is to make several small sketches in pastel and black india ink. The small-scale sketch—that is, something that can be drawn on a sketch pad page of approximately 6 by 9 inches (15 by 23 cm)—has traditionally been the artist's shorthand means of visual "notation" in which scale, movement, plan of light and dark, and so forth are tentatively indicated. In the small-sketch stage, one is more apt to try several variations on a theme, to seek out alternate design solutions, or to explore the possibilities of a new direction.

Pastels are excellent for making sketches; color can be deep or pale; they can be blended, rubbed, and superimposed. If you use some spray-fix over the pastel color, you can then work over it with black india ink. (One should use the chalk type of pastel rather than the oil-base type, which is ink-repelling.) The matrix of your black lines, or negative intervals, can be developed as well in black pastel, black conté crayon, or charcoal pencil. There are, of course, other media for developing your color sketches—watercolors, gouache, colored pencils, colored felt markers. The pastel method, though, has the advantage of being very direct and spontaneous.

MAKING THE CARTOON

You can enlarge the smaller sketch to the final size by several methods. One method is to divide your sketch into a grid and to make a corresponding grid enlarged to the full-scale size of your finished panel. Then you simply draw in full-scale size what you see in each square of the smaller grid. If the sketch is not a complex one and is not full of critical details, this method is perfectly adequate. The thing to be aware of here is that, in the process of enlarging it, you don't want to lose that certain quality the sketch may have captured.

This is an important point and deserves a bit of clarification. The value of the sketch, whether for stained glass or sculpture or painting, is fairly obvious. From a series of brief sketches we *select* one for further development and refinement. This selective process represents a kind of crucial moment in the creative process. But, as every artist knows, the next step—perhaps we should say jump—from the beguiling sketch to the "blocking out" of the proportions at full-scale is a critical one. One should be prepared to find that what had great appeal in the sketch stage may sometimes simply not "work" full-scale; in which case, more sketches should be developed. On the other hand, it might have happened that in the enlarging process you (somehow!) lost those subtle, but vital, qualities of spatial pattern, movement, rhythm, and so forth that had been caught in the sketch.

Some prefer to use an opaque (rather than a transparency) projector as an alternate method of enlarging sketches. While this process does involve the expense of the apparatus, it has certain advantages. If you are working in other media besides glass, it can be a useful addition to your studio equipment. One of the unique advantages of the projector is that you see a fairly good approximation of the full-size "effect." This has an immediacy that you do not get with the more time-consuming, gradual building-up of the grid process. (it is not so important in terms of time saved, but for the more important reason that the visual impact is quite directly perceived.) It should be emphasized that the projected sketch need not necessarily be painstakingly and unswervingly copied. It should serve as another stage to be critically looked at; changes, improvements, deletions may still be necessary.

2-9. A sketch has been enlarged to full-scale cartoon; pastels or colored chalks are used in color areas, while black paint defines the linear pattern.

You will want to project your sketch onto a white paper. First lay out the outside shape in full-scale size of your panels, using a bold, dark line so that it is easily visible. Next, tape the white paper to a wall or a large sheet of plywood fixed in an upright position. It is then a matter of moving the projector back or forth and fiddling with the focus until the projected sketch is satisfactory. Standing slightly to the side of the projected sketch, use the broad side of pastel sticks or some sort of bold-colored chalk to broadly, and rather roughly, sketch in your different areas. The idea is not to make a very exact copy of your sketch but to block-in the shapes, intervals, and movements of your sketch.

At this point, the projector has really done all it can for you. In studying your design from various distances you will be better able to see the need for further innovations or refinements.

PREPARING THE WORK SURFACE

The next step is to lay the full-scale cartoon drawing, faceup, on the flat table. (To keep the chalk or color areas from rubbing off, spray-fix your drawings. Do this spraying outdoors, if possible, since the fumes are unhealthy to breathe.) The drawing, taped onto the table, should be covered with a transparent "parting" sheet, which separates and protects your drawing from the poured epoxy. Since the sheet is transparent, you will see your design clearly as you work on it. The parting sheet can be either Mylar, polyethylene or acetate; it should be sufficiently heavy so that it will lie flat and not wrinkle too much under the weight of the slabs of glass. A thickness of approximately .007 inch (called 7 "mils" in the trade) is about right. I prefer the Mylar sheeting since it seems to be tougher, can be reused several times, and has a natural resistance to the epoxy resins. If acetate is used, a light coating of any wood wax should be rubbed over the sheet so that it will part cleanly from the epoxy. You can also use thin fiberglass sheeting for a parting sheet, but you won't be able to roll it up and store it when you are finished.

With a few pieces of masking tape holding the parting sheet in place, some strips of wood are nailed onto the work surface according to the outside dimensions of your panel. These strips of wood, which will form the outer limits of your panel, can be of the same thickness or depth to which you will pour your epoxy resin. It is recommended that the epoxy be poured to a minimum thickness of 5/8 inch (16 mm). However, if you are making smaller panels—under 2 square feet (1858 square cm)—your epoxy thickness can safely be a little thinner.

If you are laying out several panels at one time which will assemble into one window when completed, you will also nail some *horizontal* divider strips across your design to correspond to the horizontal members of the framing into which your panels will fit. Should your panel have to fit an opening which is circular or curved, use some long, thin strips of Formica veneer. Placed on edge, these will follow the curved lines of your design. They can be held in place with small blocks of wood that are lightly nailed onto the working surface.

CUTTING AND SHAPING THE GLASS

The next step is to place each piece of cut and shaped slab glass into place on the parting sheet according to your design. (The technique of using the chisel and chipping hammer to break and shape the glass is described under "Tools." It is simpler to cut and place all the glass of one color, then go on to the next color, and so forth, rather than to complete one section of the entire window at a time.

2-10. The texture, as well as the color, of the glass is best seen when held against natural light; the transparency of the glass is determined more by its physical texture than by its color.

2-11. The light box can be used to transfer shapes from pattern or cartoon to the glass with the use of a black grease pencil.

For the lighter, more transparent colors of slab glass, you can simply lay the glass blocks directly over the design, and, using a china-marking pencil, draw the shape onto the surface of the slab; this will be your guide to cutting and shaping it. For the darker colors of glass that are not so transparent and easy to see through, I recommend the following procedure: Lay a piece of clear window glass, about 1 square foot (approximately 900 square cm), on the design and, using a black grease pencil, draw the outline of the shape. Next, take the thin window glass to a light box and place the slab glass piece on top of it. You will be able to see the line well enough to draw the shape on the slab. In this case, use a red or yellow grease pencil so it will be quite visible on the surface of the dark-colored slabs.

FACETING THE GLASS

When all pieces have been cut and shaped, each shape can now be faceted. At this point you will want to consider how much faceting should be done; will all pieces be faceted or do you want to emphasize some parts of the work, leaving the balance unchipped? When doing the faceting, should you happen to chip the glass so that it is lower than the proposed epoxy level, you can build a small dam along the edge of the slab with some plasticine clay. Try to keep the clay, which is oil based, away from the *sides* of your glass.

A certain amount of faceting can be done *after* the epoxy has been poured and fully cured, rather than before. The panel should be laid flat on a table and, instead of using the chipping hammer, a long chisel should be used. Faceting after, rather than before, the pouring and curing of the epoxy is a more risky procedure, since there is always the possibility of breaking an extra-brittle piece of slab glass.

All the completed pieces of glass have now been assembled in place on the clear film over your design. My preference is to place the slabs smooth side up. The smooth side will then be on the interior, which is the principal viewing side of your panel. The "downside" of slabs, exposed to the exterior, vary greatly in texture; they are sometimes strongly patterned and pitted, depending upon the mold in which they were cast. The outside of a slab glass window is decidedly the negative side in the sense that during the day you hardly see any color of the glass from outside the building. What you do see is

the matrix grid of the epoxy surface plus the various textures of this rougher surface. I feel that the variety of these textures adds interest to the total outside appearance of the window. If the rougher side of the slabs are placed on the inside, this textural interest will be quite overpowered by the force of light and color.

2-12. Faceting is done by striking the edge of the glass with the chipping hammer.

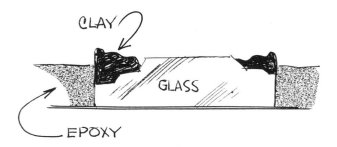

2-13. If a chip of the glass is lower than the intended epoxy level, Plasticine clay can be used to form a "protective dam." When epoxy has cured, clay is easily removed.

APPLYING THE MOLD RELEASE

Liquid latex is about the consistency of cream. It dries by the evaporation of its water content when exposed to the air. A thinly poured layer needs about 12 hours or more for drying, so it is best to plan for this to occur overnight. A fan, wafting some air over the table, will help to speed up the drying process. Also, the addition of a small amount of a solution called mold "release accelerator," supplied with the latex, will cut the drying time considerably. However, once you mix in the accelerator you must use the whole batch immediately and throw away what is left over.

Although the liquid latex can be *slightly* thinned with clean water, it must be remembered that its main job is to seep underneath each piece of glass; when it has dried, it provides an effective barrier against such seepage by the epoxy. You will notice that the latex will run under almost all the pieces of glass no matter how flat the underside may be. This is of no consequence, however, since the whole latex "skin" will be stripped away after the panel has been cured and turned over.

The latex may also be painted on *top* of each piece of slab glass; then, if you accidentally spill some epoxy on the surface of the glass during the pouring operation, it can be easily removed even after it has cured rock-hard. The latex should also be painted on the insides and top of your wood strips. This is best done first; that is, prior to pouring the latex between the glass pieces. To be on the safe side,

give the wood strips two coats of latex; the slightest bit of wood that comes in contact with the epoxy will be strongly bonded to it if unprotected. Some artists take the additionl precaution of waxing the wood first, but this is by no means a necessity.

It is of no consequence if a few dribbles of latex should happen to spill on the *sides* of your glass pieces since the latex is a very thin membrane. You will still have a watertight seal, it is colorless, and, being sealed under the epoxy, its degradation is highly improbable. However, should you ever make panels that would be placed flat, skylight fashion, and exposed to rain and possibly freezing weather, take care to keep the latex off the *sides* of your glass pieces.

If you wish to have a textured surface on the downside (exterior side) of the panel, sift dry sand, fine pebbles, or similar materials over the entire panel, about 15 to 25 minutes after the latex release agent has been poured. By that time the latex membrane should have developed just enough strength to support the weight of the texturing material.

Never use sable, bristle, or any animal hair brush for painting on the latex since these soon become clotted and are impossible to clean. Instead, get a supply of cheap, small nylon brushes. These can be washed out easily with warm water and soap. A small metal hair comb is also very useful for cleaning out the clotted latex from the brushes.

2-14. Schematic cross section showing elements in poured epoxy panel.

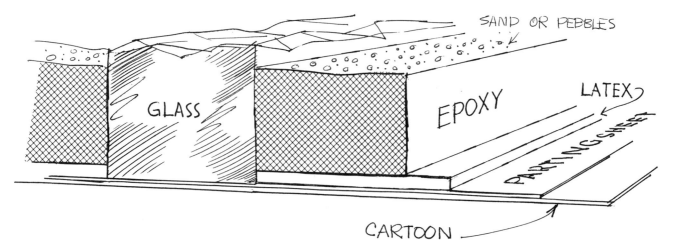

Plan the pouring of the mold release for the last operation of the day, because once you have poured it you'll want to leave the studio. The fumes, while not considered especially harmful to breathe, are obnoxious; ammonia is one of the constituents of liquid latex.

MIXING AND POURING THE EPOXY RESIN

After the mold release agent has dried, you are now ready to mix and pour the epoxy resin. Most epoxies are sold in gallon "units" consisting of two parts—the *base* and the *hardening agent* (sometimes called the "catalyst" or "curing agent"). The base is a premixed formulation of resin, fine silica sand, and coloring matter; it fills only about 80 percent of the gallon can. The hardening agent comes in a 1/2-pint can and contains about 6 ounces. The mixing of the small can of hardener with the gallon base automatically gives the right mix ratio. Should you be using less than the gallon amount, simply follow the same ratio of base-to-hardener mix. While epoxy resin formulations may vary from one manufacturer to another, precise instructions are generally supplied with the product.

It is very important that the epoxy base be thoroughly mixed *before* the hardener is added to it; it is equally important that it be mixed again *after* the hardener has been added. It would be ideal to use a paint-store type of mixer that vibrates the can furiously and does a very complete job of mixing. This is a very expensive piece of equipment, however, and is not really necessary for the small studio. With a little more effort, the 1/2-inch hand drill will do a good job. This should be a commercial- or industrial-rated heavy-duty drill with a low *rpm;* anything with less heft and power will not be as satisfactory.

Local hardware stores carry paint-mixing attachments for hand drills, but these are generally not rugged enough to do the job of mixing epoxy. Try to find a heavy-duty paint-mixing attachment at a plaster- or cement-supply center. Otherwise, if you have access to welding equipment, a simple, strong mixer, such as the one shown in the illustration can be made.

After prying the top off the gallon can, use a spatula to scrape any excess from the lid back into the contents. Before the hardener has been added, the epoxy is a dense, heavily viscous mass and the various elements in it may tend to settle and stratify at the bottom of the can, particularly after it has been stored for some time. It is also affected by the cold (due to shipping or storing conditions) and may appear to have crystallized somewhat at the lower sediment level. In this case, warm it gradually in an oven or double boiler, *never* allowing the heat to climb above what you consider to be a hot-bath temperature; then mix it thoroughly.

Mix the epoxy until all the lumps have been broken up and it is of an even consistency. In order to get a complete mix, scrape down the sides of the can. This is easily done if you take off the upper lip of the gallon can. Do this with a heavy-duty can opener or with a large, sharp hunting knife, which will cut through the metal as you tap it along with a hammer.

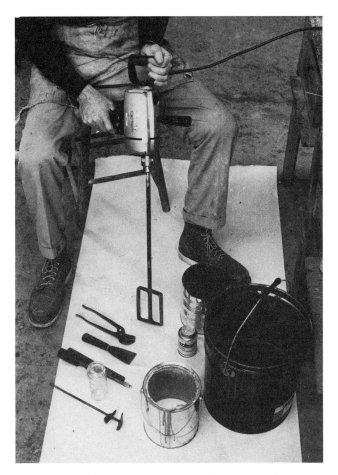

2-15. A heavy-duty mixing attachment is necessary when working with 5-gallon units of epoxy. For better control, the epoxy is best mixed 1 gallon at a time.

You are now ready to add the hardener. If you are using the hand drill for mixing, you must keep the can from whirling about while the mixer is stirring it. This is readily accomplished by sitting down and bracing the can with your feet. Just before you complete the mixing, scrape down the sides of the can with a long spatula, being certain that the epoxy and hardener are well mixed; unmixed material will never harden.

The mixed resin is now ready to be poured. It will help to squeeze the top of the can so that it forms a pouring spout. Another method is to pour half of the contents into a clean coffee can, which is also "spouted" on one side; this will give you more control and aim when pouring. The whole mixing and pouring routine should be one continuous operation. Time, tide, and epoxy wait for no man, which is to say that the resin begins to set up within less than 1/2 hour; if several panels are to be poured at one time, as well as textured with sand, interruptions (having to look around for this tool or that, for example) can be very disconcerting. A simple checklist of necessary items is useful just before beginning the mixing of epoxy—mineral spirits, several spatulas, rags, knife, large can opener, gloves, hammer, screwdriver or lid pry, sand, or pebbles.

2-16. The epoxy resin must be thoroughly mixed before, as well as after, the hardener has been added. The 1/2-inch, heavy-duty hand drill with low rpm is very useful for this.

2-17. For smaller panels, the epoxy can be carefully measured and mixed in 1-gallon units and then poured from a "spouted" coffee can.

Precautions. Epoxy resins are potent skin irritants, and, while sensitivity to them varies from one individual to another, continual care must be taken to keep the stuff off the skin and, especially, out of the eyes.

Frequent washings with soap and water followed by the application of a hand lotion are recommended. Wearing rubber gloves when working with epoxy is also a sound, general precaution. There are some people, however, with skins that are particularly sensitive to the additional sweating of the hands caused by prolonged use of the rubber gloves; this in itself can cause some irritation. It is recommended that they apply several applications of lanolin or a glycerin-based lotion before handling epoxy, followed by a thorough soap-and-water washing when finished. It is very bad practice to use such studio solvents as mineral spirits, lacquer thinner, acetone, and so forth on your skin, even if you wash immediately thereafter. The simplest rule is to stay with the soap-water-and-lotion routine.

Many products, including epoxy, are subject to the Consumer Product Safety Act, which specifies that the product may be purchased for industrial use only, rather than for "use in a home environment." This is another indication that such materials can be injurious to health unless handled with care and common sense; above all, these materials should never be stored where children could get at them.

Calculating Epoxy Needs. When calculating the amount of epoxy to order for a specific project, you must first estimate the approximate percentage of *glass* in your total design. The following table shows the coverage obtained with 1 gallon of epoxy resin when cast at various depths:

SQUARE FEET OF PANEL COVERAGE PER GALLON UNIT OF EPOXY

GLASS PERCENTAGE	THICKNESS OF EPOXY CAST				
	1/2"	5/8"	3/4"	7/8"	1"
30%	4.03	3.23	2.69	2.30	2.01
40%	4.70	3.77	3.13	2.68	2.35
50%	5.64	4.52	3.76	3.22	2.82
60%	7.05	5.65	4.70	4.03	3.53

(Table courtesy of Thermoset Plastics, Indianapolis, Ind.)

Here's an example: A project consisting of eight faceted glass windows, each panel measuring 2 by 3 feet, totals 48 square feet. With a 40 percent glass estimate and epoxy poured to a desired thickness of 5/8-inch, you will get 3.77 square feet per gallon; 48 square feet divided by 3.77 equals 12.72 gallons, or 13 gallons. Thus, you should order 15 gallons, the additional 2 being a safety factor to allow for possible wastage or variation in the percentage of glass area estimated.

TEXTURING THE EPOXY RESIN

The epoxy can be textured as soon as the surface of the resin will support the weight of the sand, pebbles, or other material you may be using. The untextured epoxy tends to cure with a shiny, glossy-looking surface that is not particularly attractive. There are several types of sand, different in color and in fineness, as well as variegated small pebbles, or a combination of both that can be experimented with. But, whatever the material you choose for texturing, it should be well dried of its moisture content before it is used.

There will inevitably have to be a certain amount of cleaning up of drips or blobs of epoxy that have fallen on the edges of your glass pieces. This is best done with a bit of mineral spirits on a rag immediately after pouring the epoxy; once it has hardened, it is very difficult to remove.

The best procedure is to schedule the pouring operation toward the end of the day, since the fumes from the epoxy resins are quite strong and should not be breathed for any extended length of time without adequate ventilation. A portable fan is handy to keep the fumes from rising directly into your face during the pouring operation.

There is an alternate method of texturing the downside of a faceted glass panel. This involves sprinkling a layer of fine sand, about 1/8 inch deep (approximately 3mm), over and between the assembled slab glass pieces after they are all arranged in position on your design. The latex form release is thus not needed, except that the form release should still be painted on the wood frame that forms the perimeter of the panel. The epoxy resin is then mixed, poured, and allowed to cure, as already described. When cured, the panel can be turned over and the excess sand brushed away. A second batch of a smaller amount of epoxy is then prepared and poured between the glass on the second side of the panel. Again, a thin layer of sand or similar texturing material is evenly sifted and scattered over the entire surface. After the epoxy is cured, the panel is then swept clean of the excess sand. Although the step of pouring the latex mold release is eliminated, two mixings, pourings, and curings of the epoxy are necessary in this method. However, a complete control of the texturing effect or the use of unusual texturing materials can be obtained by this particular technique.

2-18. Faceted glass panels can be textured with sand, pebbles, or marble powders immediately after the epoxy has been poured. After the epoxy has cured, the excess sand or texturing material is brushed off with a whisk broom.

THE CURING PROCESS

The panel should cure for 4 to 6 hours at a temperature of 70 to 80 degrees Fahrenheit (21 to 27 degrees Centigrade) before being moved or worked on in any way. Should you then need the table space to start another panel, the panel should be slid carefully onto another flat surface and left to cure further; the parting sheet should still be adhered to the downside. At this stage the panel should never be subjected to any flexing, strain, or uneven support. The use of a curing rack thus allows the work table to be used twice in one day, if necessary. The full curing process should take from 3 to 4 days, with the panel stored flat, at a temperature of at least 70 degrees Fahrenheit (21 degrees Centigrade); allow the full curing time before installing the panel. It is important to pour the epoxy at these warmer temperatures because as the temperature drops below approximately 70 degrees Fahrenheit (22 degrees Centigrade) the curing slows down and more time is needed for a thorough cure. To be on the safe side, carefully check the manufacturer's directions.

Note: It is estimated that 4 to 5 days curing time at 77 degrees Fahrenheit (25 degrees Centigrade) will produce approximately 98 percent of the ultimate strength. If it should be necessary to have panels finished in a shorter period of time, heat lamps or ovens may be used to speed up the curing time. Heating for 2 to 3 hours at temperatures near 200 degrees Fahrenheit (94 degrees Centigrade) or 6 to 8 hours at 150 to 175 degrees Fahrenheit (approximately 66 to 79 degrees Centigrade) will produce a complete cure. Heat *should not be* applied until the resin has first gelled at room temperature to a tack-free state.

FINISHING THE PANELS

After they have cured for at least 8 hours, you can strip the latex mold release from the back of your panel; but it must still be allowed to cure for 3 days lying flat. When turning over the panel, care must be taken not to impose too great a strain on any one corner of the panel. If it is of large size, it will be heavy, and a two-man operation may be safest. If the wood base on which the panel has been cast is movable, it can be upended on one side without putting any strain on the panel. Otherwise, the panel will have to be carefully pried up, with special care taken to pry always at two points; any strain on the

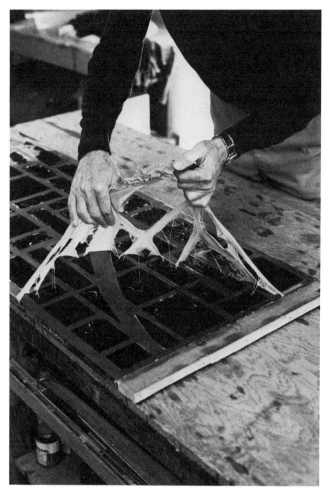

panel, therefore, will be distributed more evenly. The clear parting sheet can then be stripped off the panel. Some of the latex will still be in a liquid state and this should be left to dry. After it dries, it can easily be pulled off the entire panel.

If, for some reason, the sand texture or color of the exterior side of the panel is uneven or you wish to change the color, lay the panel flat, face down, and paint a thin layer of *clear*, laminating epoxy on the epoxy areas only. (See Chapter 5.) Care must be taken that none of the clear epoxy gets on your glass areas. When the whole panel has been coated, a fine sand or marble dust of the right color can be sifted and evenly scattered over it. After it has cured for about 24 hours, the excess sand is then brushed off.

2-19. After curing, the panel is turned over and the latex mold release is stripped from the back of the panel.

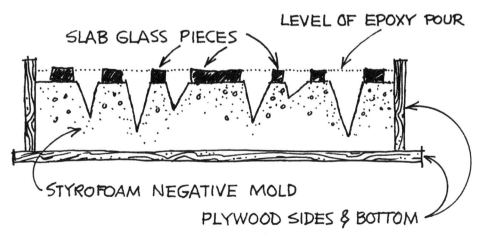

LEVEL OF EPOXY POUR

SLAB GLASS PIECES

STYROFOAM NEGATIVE MOLD

PLYWOOD SIDES & BOTTOM

2-20. Schematic diagram for casting dimensional slab glass panels.

2-22. Faceted slab glass used in the form of a wall, rather than as a "window," the work is unusual in its graphic flow of the curving black lines; about three different thicknesses of lines are used, contrasting strongly with the heavy vertical support columns. Example shown is from the Warren State Hospital in Warren, Pennsylvania, and was done by the Willet Studios. (Photo by the Willet Studios)

2-21. Walls of slab glass with a three-dimensional effect can be achieved by casting epoxy on a carved Styrofoam mold. The photograph shows Don Shepherd's treatment of a baptistry wall in Sacred Heart Church, Eureka, California. In this example the slab glass is not faceted, but presents a flat, flush surface within the projecting strips of epoxy. (Courtesy Don Shepherd)

2-23. Detail of a faceted glass window by Jean Jacques Duval showing the "pictorial" quality that can be achieved solely by the shaping of each piece of glass. The epoxy matrix forms the black lines as well as the black areas. The window is in Cardinal Spellman High School, Bronx, New York. (Courtesy of the artist)

CHAPTER 3.

FACETED GLASS IN CONCRETE

Concrete is a much more available and far less expensive material than epoxy resin. It is attractively elemental in nature—cement, sand, pebbles, water —as compared to the exotic formulations of epoxy. Glass in concrete has a rugged, massive quality and integrates beautifully into many contemporary structures. It is also adaptable to a variety of textural finishes.

All, however, is not wine and roses when it comes to working with concrete. If any enduring results are to be attained, a much longer curing time will be required, and, if reinforcement is needed, it must be done right. (Panels smaller than approximately 2 square feet may safely be made without reinforcement.)

CUTTING AND LAYING THE SLAB GLASS

The procedure for cutting and laying the pattern of the individual slab glass pieces is almost the same as it would be if you were making an epoxy pour instead of a concrete casting. The only difference will be that you will not want to lay the pieces of glass any closer together than about 1/2 inch (1.3 cm). Concrete panels also require some form of reinforcing, and sufficient space must be left for this. Concrete has a much lower strength than epoxy. A typical sidewalk mix, for example, has a compressive strength of approximately 3,000

3-1. Example of a massive wall pierced with faceted glass set in concrete at St. Mary's Priory in Lancashire, England. (Courtesy of Architect Weightman)

3-2. View of curved wall of Chapel of Meditation in Lancashire, England, showing interesting "negative" pattern of faceted glass set in concrete. Note large size of cast units, which, if not site cast, must be specially designed to be transportable. (Courtesy of Architect Weightman)

pounds per square inch (approximately 1,360 kg per 6.45 cm²). The compressive strength of concrete is the measure of its ability to withstand pressures in pounds per square inch under laboratory test conditions. The epoxy formulated for use in casting slab glass has a compressive strength of approximately 12,800 pounds per square inch (5,805 kg per 6.45 cm²). Flexural and tensile differences between the two are in similar proportions. (*Note:* Very wide ranges are possible in the specific designs of both concrete and epoxy resins; concrete compressive strengths can be designed anywhere in the range of 2,000 to 10,000 pounds per square inch (900 to 4,500 kg per 6.45 square cm); epoxies can be formulated in the range of 3,000 to 30,000 pounds per square inch (1,360 to 13,600 kg per 6.45 square cm).

3-3. Roger Darricarrere shown in his Los Angeles foundry pouring molten glass into deep molds for eventual use in concrete and sculpture. (Courtesy of the artist)

PREPARING THE REINFORCEMENT

Heavy galvanized wire (impervious to rust), which you have welded or wired well together, will be adequate reinforcement for smaller panels. (*Note:* The fumes from welding galvanized metals are toxic; use adequate ventilation.) For larger panels, use 1/4-inch or 1/2-inch reinforcing bars. Try to keep your reinforcing grid high enough off the table so that it is in the middle of the thickness of your panel. For this use some small concrete stilts or some polyethylene "chairs," as they are called in the trade.

Make sure you have treated the wood strips of your borders and dividers with a concrete "release agent," such as linseed oil, wax, or brushed-on latex. Tapered horizontal divider strips can be removed more easily than those with parallel sides. If you want a textured surface for the downside of your panels, scatter a layer of sand, pebbles, or similar material evenly over the entire layout. This layer can be about 1/8 inch thick (3 mm).

MIXING THE CONCRETE

You are now ready to mix a batch of concrete for your casting. Premix all the dry ingredients thoroughly; then gradually add and mix in the water, but only enough water to make the mixture flowable. Here, an important rule is this: The less water you can use and still achieve a workable mixture—that is, one that will flow—the stronger your finished piece will be. A general recipe for mixing concrete is the "1-2-3" combination; that is, one part dry portland cement, two parts sand, and three parts aggregate, (all volume measures). For this type of concrete work, the aggregate, or pebbles, need be no larger than 1/4 inch (7 mm). For the type of portland cement to use, you can specify type I, type I-P, or, for more rapid curing, type III.

Concrete can be colored or tinted with admixtures of mortar black or earth colors. Color is best when well mixed with the cement in the dry state—before the water is added. You can never accurately judge what the eventual color will be unless you take the time to make a small experimental batch in advance; the mix has to have sufficient curing time to be judged for color, otherwise it may not match your final panels.

Alternate Mixes. A *mortar* mix can also be used; that is, the same ingredients as listed above, but without the larger aggregate (pebbles). A mix of one part cement to two parts dry sand, (volume measurements) is adequate. Again, use a minimum amount of water. This is a much more manageable mixture, though slightly less strong than it would be with the addition of the aggregate.

Terms. To clear up some of the terminology, *cement* is the dry powder that is sold as portland cement; *mortar* is the cement-plus-sand mixture that is used in bricklaying; *concrete* is both of these with the addition of coarser aggregate (pebbles or small, crushed rock).

It is called "portland" because the mixture, which was patented in England in 1824, resembles a natural stone found on the "Isle of Portland." The Romans of the empire were master workers in concrete, but the practice was lost in the Dark Ages. The pre-Columbian civilizations of the Maya and Aztec were incredibly versatile and imaginative in their use of a kind of "stucco," which is a variety of cement work.

3-4. Roger Darricarrere's sculptured panels of faceted glass set in reinforced concrete in Our Lady of Lourdes Catholic Church, Tujunga, California. Panels are cast in frames of 1 1/2-inch steel angle frames; the reinforcing is welded to frames and the frames are welded to structural steel. Thick glass is cut and shaped with a diamond-blade lapidary saw.

3-5. Detail of Roger Darricarrere's 27-foot-high concrete relief casting for Our Lady of Lourdes Church. Some of the relief projects to 8 inches; concrete was cast over a Styrofoam form. The thickness of the concrete is a minimum of 1 1/4 inches. (Courtesy of the artist).

Portland cement comes in white and the usual "concrete gray," as well as in buff color. It is available in a variety of types, which are adaptable to the specific engineering needs of the job, but, unless you will be doing large-scale projects in concrete, they are only of peripheral interest to the artist. There are, for example, such things as "high early-strength" concrete and "air-entrained" concrete, to name but two of a variety of versatile adaptions in concrete. Further references on the subject can be found in the Annual Reference Guide issue of *Concrete Construction Magazine,* as listed in the Bibliography.

There are also very useful admixtures, such as *pozzolan,* which strengthen the mass, workability, and general character of concrete. These should be definitely considered and are available from your local concrete dealer.

POURING THE CONCRETE

Start in the middle of the panel and work out to the edges, pouring to the maximum thickness as you go. Use fingers, palette knife, or small wooden sticks to direct and even out the flow of the concrete.

To settle the poured panel and to release trapped air bubbles, tap a hammer on the table around the frame. This will set off a vibration which settles the pour, and will cause the mix to flow into any cavities that may be below the surface. This vibrating need not be overdone, since too much tends to separate the mix; heavier aggregates go to the bottom, displacing water, which gathers on the surface. If an excess of water "bleeds" to the surface, it can be sopped up with some toweling or blotters. Generally, a "laitance," as it is called in concrete work, is formed on the surface; that is, a layer of portland-cement-and-water forms paste. If a professional vibrating device is used or if you devise some other similar rig, watch the tendency to overdo the vibrating. One advantage in working with concrete is that there is no great urge to rush, which there can be with the quicker-setting epoxy resin. After an hour or two, the surface of the concrete can still be textured or some embedments can be pressed in. Some previous experimentation with this kind of texturing, however, is a must. A *light* sprinkling of fine sand can be sifted over the laitance, but it is not good practice to sift dry cement over the surface, since the added cement does not get uniformly

mixed with the aggregate and water, making a nonhomogeneous, imperfectly cured surface.

There are two main alternate ways to ensure that your cast concrete or mortar mix will not seep under the glass pieces and obscure your design:

1. You can follow the exact same procedure done in the latex mold release system for epoxy panels.
2. You can lay your entire arrangement of glass pieces on a bedding of foam rubber, approximately 1/4 to 1/2 inch thick (7 to 13 mm).

With the second method, the weight of your glass pieces depresses the foam pad and keeps the cast mix from running under the glass. With this system, however, you cannot "see" your pattern so well as you can through the transparent sheeting used for epoxy panels; should you accidentally bump a piece of glass in the casting process, you're in trouble. You can, however, paste each piece of glass into position with something like rubber cement. All things considered, the latex mold release system seems simpler and better.

In glass in concrete panels you can obtain two quite different effects:

1. Casting the concrete mix just to the thickness of the depth of the glass chunks. This gives a fairly flush panel on both sides.
2. You can make a panel in which the glass slab pieces are considerably "inset" below the level of the casting, as if each different color of glass occupied its own shallow "window."

The second is an interesting technique that is used with great results by the master glassworker, Jacques Loire, of France. (Incidentally, as a technique, glass in concrete seems to be more favored in Europe, where it was first developed, than in the United States.) The "inset" process results in thicker and heavier panels. The use of Plasticine clay on the upside of your glass pieces permits the deeper casting of concrete.

Professional concrete people generally speak of "placing" concrete, since they hardly ever use a mixture with so much water content as to be called

3-6. This 10- by 12-foot screen of faceted glass set in concrete by Roger Darricarrere was done for a bank in California. The panels have a strongly sculptural feeling. In some areas the glass is 5 inches in thickness; certain areas of the glass have been laminated together with epoxy. The whole assemblage is set in a matrix of welded-reinforced concrete. The screen is back-lit with fluorescent tubes. (Courtesy of the artist)

"pourable." The viscosity of concrete is referred to as "slump." The term is derived from the process of placing a sample of a freshly mixed batch into a truncated cone; when the cone is carefully lifted off, the sample slumps to its own natural profile. Less water in the mix gives a low slump reading; more water gives a high slump index.

THE CURING PROCESS

Panels *must* be kept damp during the curing period. Covering the panels with polyethylene sheeting and checking every day to see that they are not drying too rapidly is a good practice. A daily sprinkling with water may be necessary to prevent undue evaporation of moisture. Allow a week to 10 days for damp curing of panels.

If the panels have to be moved before they are fully cured, this should be done carefully to avoid cracking them. For example, if you want an exposed aggregate finish on the downside (or outside) of the panels, they should be turned over along their longest edge about 8 hours after the casting. The outer layer of concrete can then be scrubbed with a wire brush and hosed down until the layer of aggregate is evenly exposed. Muriatic acid can also be used for this operation, care being taken to give the panel a final and thorough rinsing with water. (*Note:* Muriatic acid is highly caustic; always wear goggles and rubber gloves when working with it.) Be sure to continue the day-to-day curing of the panels, however. It bears repeating that advance experimentation with this process is recommended due to the variables of working conditions, temperature, and materials used.

If a large project makes it necessary to work on panels outdoors, it is important to prevent the panels from being damaged by temperature extremes. For example, freezing temperatures are fatal to concrete that has not fully cured, and the eventual strength of the concrete will be considerably lessened. There are no admixtures that retard frost, despite advertising claims to the contrary. However, an admixture of calcium chloride can accelerate the *rate* of strength gain, thus making the concrete less susceptible to damage from freezing in the earliest hours of its life.

3-7. Wood sculpture in laminated walnut with faceted glass by Roger Darricarrere. Located in a California bank, it measures 13 feet long by 3 feet high. (Photo by Richard Gross)

At the other extreme, hot, dry weather means that the work *must* be kept damp during the curing time, since moisture content evaporating too rapidly will also adversely affect the strength of the finished piece.

VARIATIONS

There are many other variations possible with the faceted slab glass in concrete process. One example is casting concrete onto a smooth bed of damp sand with pieces of thick glass embedded slightly into the sand. Another is casting concrete onto a Plasticine (oil base) clay that has been patterned, sculpted, or textured in the areas around strategically placed glass chunks. Experiment thoroughly, however, before launching into any serious work.

3-9. Don Shepherd works on negative Styrofoam forms for large concrete castings with embedments of rocks and glass chunks. (Photo by Vytautas Mazelis, Ridgewood, N.Y.)

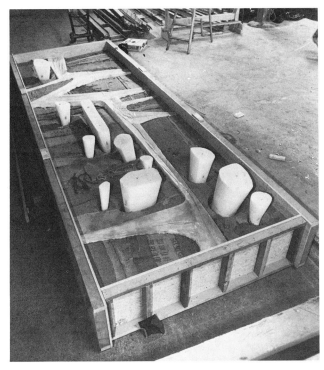

3-8. Don Shepherd works in massive scale with concrete and faceted slab glass. The photograph shows one of the negative molds for 24-foot wall panels for Ascension Church in Hamden, Connecticut. (For appearance of finished panels see color illustration 23.) Varieties of surface textures were achieved with areas of polyvinyl plus burlap bags plus ropes, all glued in place so as not to move. After the curing of concrete, Styrofoam shapes were pushed out and thick glass pieces were set in openings. (Photo by Jack Stock Studio, Derby, Conn.)

When set in concrete, larger pieces of faceted glass sometimes crack after the work has been finished and installed in place. It is not known whether this is caused by erratic curing or by the temperature extremes of some climates. As a safeguard, there is a way to "cushion," as well as to seal, each piece of glass; a bitumen or asphaltic mixture is painted around the *edges* of the glass pieces before they are put into position on the design. This thin layer of bitumen provides a small, but sufficient, factor to make up for the different expansion and contraction coefficients of glass and concrete. The

black color of the bitumen will not be noticed in the finished work.

The foregoing is essentially a summary of the major "dos and don'ts" of working with concrete. Inevitably, new demands, and thus new questions, about the best concrete techniques will be posed whenever this ancient material is used as an art medium. For this reason it is good practice to seek out the advice of those who have had long experience with concrete, either working directly with it or selling supplies to the trade.

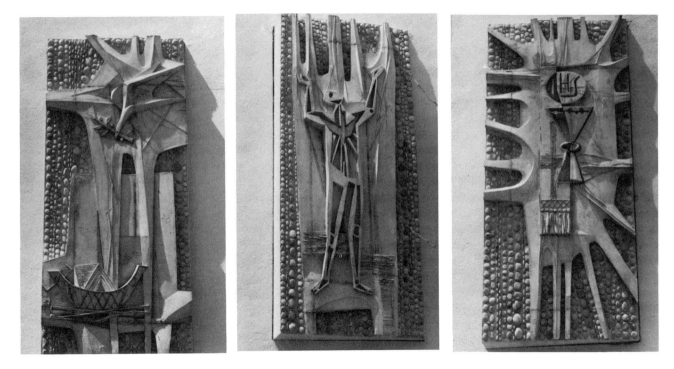

3-10. Three of a series of concrete panels by Don Shepherd in cast concrete on Styrofoam molds. Panels measure 10 feet tall and weigh approximately 7,000 pounds. (Photo by the artist)

3-11. Experimental panels by Don Shepherd using stone, burlap,
metal bars, and textured sands on one side with direct expression
in fresh concrete on the other. (Photo by the artist)

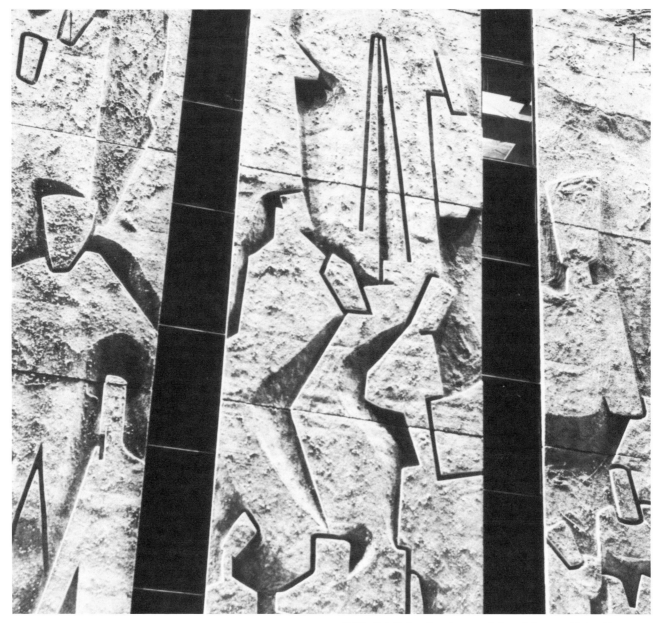

3-12. Detail showing deep sculptured shapes obtained in precast concrete panels using plastic-foam forms. Pozzolith, a water-reducing, set-controlling admixture was used to help minimize shrinkage and provide high early strength for safe handling of the panels. Work was done for the Professional Arts Center in Miami, Florida. The sculptor is Albert S. Vrana. (Courtesy of Master Builders, Cleveland, Ohio)

3-13. The main facade of the Provincial Administration Building of Bloemfontein, South Africa, consists entirely of large precast panels of faceted glass in concrete. The sculptured effect of the concrete shapes are emphasized by their projecting slightly beyond the surrounding surfaces of the colored slab glass. Photo courtesy of Saint Gobain Industries, Paris.

CHAPTER 4.

WORKING WITH LEADED GLASS

In stained glass work, or leaded glass, the sequence of steps, from start to finish, can generally be divided as follows:
1. Making the design.
2. Making the cartoon.
3. Making the pattern.
4. Cutting the pattern.
5. Cutting the glass to the pattern.
6. Preparing the work surface.
7. Assembling the leads and glass.
8. Soldering.
9. Puttying and cleaning.

TYPES OF GLASS
There is considerable difference in the kinds of glass that are used for leaded glass work. They are divided into types according to the method of manufacture, which determines their texture, transparency or opacity, as well as their singularity of color.

Antique Glass. A wide variety of colored glasses are available for stained glass work; they vary in color, transparency, and texture. The most beautiful of the whole range of colored glass are the ones called "antique." Despite the name, antique glass is not old. It is called antique because it is still made today by the ancient process of blowing a blob of molten glass into a large elongated bottle shape which is then trimmed at both ends. The resulting cylinder is cut lengthwise and allowed to flatten out and cool. Thus, it is not generally of a uniform thickness; it has streaks, ripples, and occasional bubbles that add delightful variations to the light that it transmits.

Cathedral Glass. This is a term that covers a variety of machine-made, flat-rolled colored glasses that are frequently textured on one side. Some of these are named: hammered, rippled, seedy, marine and double-rolled smooth. All of these textured glasses should be cut on the smooth side. Cathedral glass is much less expensive than antique glass and is available in an extensive range of colors.

Opalescent Glass. A semiopaque glass of milky or marbleized appearance is called opalescent. It was used extensively in Victorian art glass work. It is somewhat brittle and a bit tricky to cut.

Flashed Glass. This is a clear base of glass that has been stained with a thin layer of color on one side while still in the molten state. In etched or sandblasted glass work the thin color layer is removed, allowing the clear or frosted glass to show in the form of a design. Flashed glass is always cut on the clear side and etched or sandblasted on the colored side.

Frosted Glass. Frosted or obscure glass (as used in shower partitions), heat-absorbent glass, or tinted or tempered glass is infrequently used in art work. Most are tricky to cut and are expensive.

OBTAINING THE GLASS

One of the best sources for obtaining small quantities of glass are stained glass studios, which are listed in the telephone yellow pages in most larger towns and cities. "Scrap glass," frequently in large enough pieces to suit your purposes, can be bought, or, if the studio happens to be well-stocked, you can buy larger sheets. Some commercial glass-and-paint supply-centers may carry a stock of cathedral glass, but the selection of colors is generally very limited.

Considerable money can be saved if you order directly from stained-glass supply-houses, but most of them will only accept orders of sizeable amounts. Here "cooperative" buying with the help of fellow stained-glass enthusiasts can be very advantageous.

TOOLS

If you are just getting started in stained glass work, you will be pleasantly surprised at the low cost and availability of the basic tools required. But there are some specialized tools which the serious student will eventually want to acquire. The whole range of stained glass tools will be described here; your budget will be your guide. Guidance on how to use each tool is given under "Making a Leaded Glass Panel."

Glass Cutter. This tool, which is available at all hardware stores, is one of those rarities of modern life—a simple tool that has not been improved upon for several generations that is still inexpensive. It will perform any kind of straight or curved cuts you may need. Essentially, it is a small, hard metal wheel, set into a brass bearing, with a handle to grasp it. The diamond-tipped cutter is a more expensive, yet much less maneuverable, instrument. It is tricky to use when cutting curved shapes; it is mostly used in the glass trade for cutting thick plate and commercial glass and is generally used for straight cuts, rather than curves. One of its advantages is that it lasts indefinitely.

Glass cutters come in various degrees of metal wheel hardness. For general purposes try a Fletcher 06 or Red Devil; they are most suitable for cutting art glass and hard-surfaced opalescent glass. When the glass cutter gets dull it can be resharpened, but after a couple of sharpenings it should be discarded for a new one. There are several varieties of handle shapes available from different manufacturers; experimentation will soon tell you your own preference. The steel-wheel glass cutter is probably the most versatile instrument for cutting art glass; the tungsten wheel, which is harder and much more long lasting is sometimes blamed for making a coarser, rather than a delicate, cut. Again, a great deal depends on "touch," or the individual way one uses an instrument.

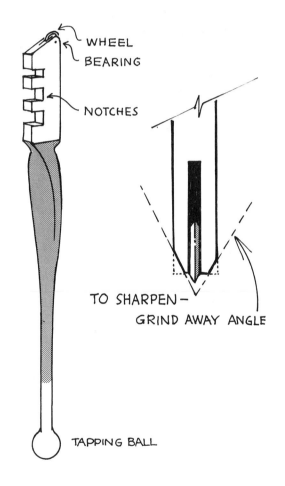

4-1. The glass cutter.

Glazing Knife. This is a necessary item that performs a number of functions. Glazing knives come in several forms, starting with the low-cost type that you can make yourself to the more expensive professional knife. Because they are used in cutting the lead cames, they must have a thin blade and a very sharp edge. You can make your own from a putty knife that has a thin, strong, stiff blade (*not* the flexible type of blade). The length of the handle can be cut down, the blade being ground down and shaped to a curved edge, as shown in the illustration. The curved edge allows you to rock the blade when cutting leads and, if kept sharpened, the thin steel edge will not tend to crush the lead out of shape. A heavy-duty mat knife with replaceable blades can also be used provided that a whetstone is kept handy to maintain the edge. Many professional art glass-workers favor the crescent-shaped glazing knife. They have a substantial feeling in the hand and are made of fine steel, but must be kept razor sharp. The curved shape permits a rocking action when cutting the leads. (Do not confuse this knife with a linoleum-cutting knife which has the sharp edge on the inner, rather than the outer, crescent.)

4-2. For the cutting of lead cames knives must be kept very sharp; the lead is easily crushed by a dull blade. When "adapting" linoleum knife, outer edge of curve must be sharpened. (Inner edge will not be of much use in stained glass work.)

There are other variations for cutting lead cames that are worth mentioning. "Industrial type" single-edge razor blades are inexpensive when bought in quantity; being very sharp and thin, they make a very accurate cut in lead cames, but must be thrown away after they've been used a few times. An artist I know makes use of a small band saw with a thin blade for cutting and mortising the lead cames.

Soldering Iron. Available in most hardware stores or supply houses, a 100-watt model is generally recommended. There are many smaller types of soldering irons on the market, but these are more for delicate electrical soldering and are not up to the needs of stained glass work. A tip with a diameter of 3/8 to 1/2 inch is best for general stained glass soldering.

The electrical soldering gun, a more expensive tool, is prized by some, though not all, glass craftsmen. They are quick-heating, have a high-low trigger control, automatically shut off when not being used, and don't require a stand since they can be safely placed on their side. In addition, soldering guns have tips that can reach into small areas, localizing the heat.

Preferences in soldering irons vary greatly from one person to another. Before buying the iron, or soldering gun, try, if possible, to visit a stained glass shop so that you may ask some questions about the various types available.

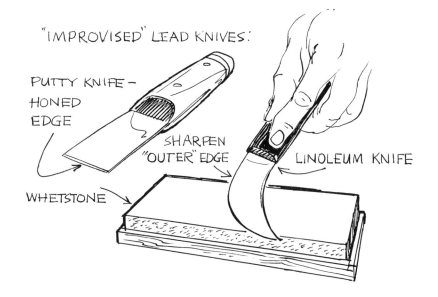

"IMPROVISED" LEAD KNIVES:

PUTTY KNIFE —
HONED
EDGE

SHARPEN
"OUTER" EDGE

LINOLEUM KNIFE

WHETSTONE

Pattern Shears. You will need some means of cutting a paper pattern that will remove a thin strip of space from your pattern when you cut. This is for the space that will be taken up by the "heart" of the lead cames. An ingenious device for this purpose is the pattern shears. They can be fairly expensive items, depending upon the brand; buy the best one that you can afford, since they are essential to doing any kind of serious stained glass work. If you can't afford the pattern shears, an inexpensive substitute can be made from single-edge razor blades. Tape two of these together, with a thin cardboard or wood spacer between the blades. If this homemade cutter is held so that both blades get even pressure when cutting they will perform quite well. Still another alternative is to purchase a device called a "dual-line cutter."

Lead Came Stretcher. Before you use lead cames in a stained glass panel, they must be stretched from their limp, curved state to a more rigid, straight one. Any sort of bench vise will suffice, provided it is well anchored into place. Lacking this, convenient and inexpensive lead vises are available from supply houses.

Lathekin. This tool is used mainly for running down the channel of lead, opening it up so that it will accept the glass shapes easily. The lathekin is generally a homemade item fashioned from a piece of hardwood, with a large enough handle to fit your grasp.

Stopping Knife. This can be made from any blunt-edged knife; it is used for such things as straightening out lead flanges. A large-handled oyster knife with blunted edges makes a good fit in your hand. A bent kitchen knife, the blade being bent only at a slight angle and not pointed or sharp, will be useful for inserting the glass into the lead cames.

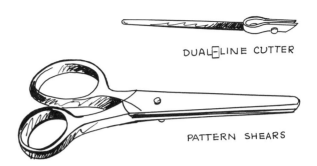

DUAL-LINE CUTTER

PATTERN SHEARS

4-3. Pattern shears, or other devices such as dual-line cutters are needed to cut out the pattern.

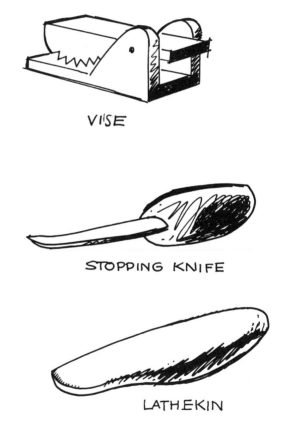

VISE

STOPPING KNIFE

LATHEKIN

4-4. A vise, stopping knife, and lathekin are needed to work with lead cames.

Pliers. Ordinary household pliers can be used in stained glass work, but the advantages of the professional "grozing" pliers are that they are precision made of untempered steel and have a bite that exerts an even pressure on the top and bottom sides of the glass; they are less apt to crack the edge of the glass when pressure is applied. The most useful pliers for general stained glass work have jaws about 1/2 inch across. Round-nosed pliers are useful for trimming small pieces of glass from an irregular edge or for attempting difficult "inside" cuts. Plate pliers have wide gripping edges and are useful when dealing with the heavier 1/4-inch plate glass.

Miscellaneous Tools. An oilstone is essential for keeping your tools sharp. A supply of nails, approximately the 1 1/2-inch common type but, preferably, horseshoe or "farrier's" nails, will be needed to keep the glass pieces of your design in position until you are ready for soldering. A bench brush, dustpan, large scrub brush, and such drafting supplies as a T square and triangle, a straightedge (at least 18 inches long), a compass, masking tape, pushpins, a china-marking pencil, and some hard and soft-grade pencils will be needed. You will also need a small, lightweight hammer, such as the double-headed tack hammer, and a carpenter's square of approximately 16 by 24 inches (40 by 60cm) is most useful. You should have a drawing board, as large as you can afford, to be used only for laying out your designs and a separate flat work board of 1/2 or 3/4 inch (12 to 18mm) with the edges well-sanded. The work board will receive much nailing, staining, and rough usage.

MATERIALS
In addition to glass and various tools, several materials will be needed to bond the lead and glass.

Lead. The harmony of lead and glass is one of the enduring marvels of art. A stained glass window is held together with lead channels called "cames" (spelled calmes in Great Britain). Medieval artisans found that lead was readily workable, available, inexpensive, and very durable in comparison to most ferrous metals. Not only does it perform a structural role, but the leading provides an interesting web of black lines between colors.

Lead cames are available in many configurations; until you've had some practice making several stained glass projects, however, it is recommended that you buy only two sizes—1/4 inch and 3/8 inch (5 and 8mm) flat leads. The 3/8-inch leads are generally sold in 6-foot lengths (1.8m); the 1/4-inch leads are sold in rolls and are priced by the pound. A certain amount of lead will inevitably be wasted in usage, and this should be considered when you order supplies. Unused leads should be wrapped in paper when stored for any length of time to avoid oxidation of the lead surface.

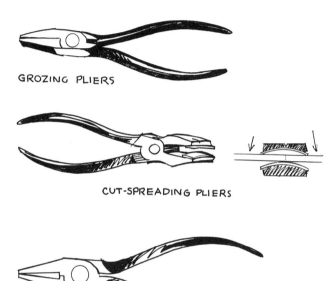

GROZING PLIERS

CUT-SPREADING PLIERS

GLASS PLIERS

4-5. Grozing pliers are flat-nosed, "soft" pliers used to "groze," or nibble away, any splinters or small pieces of glass that have remained after the glass is scored and broken. If they cannot be found at your supply source, grozers can be made from flat-nosed pliers that have been heated to take the temper out of the jaws.

Cut-spreading pliers are not a necessary item but are very useful especially for cutting long, narrow strips of glass. The jaws produce an equal pressure on both sides of the score, giving a clean, straight break.

Glass pliers, which have angled jaws for gripping the glass, are used mainly for dealing with glass shapes that are too small or oddly-shaped to be gripped by the fingers. Jaw widths can vary from 1/4 inch to a full inch.

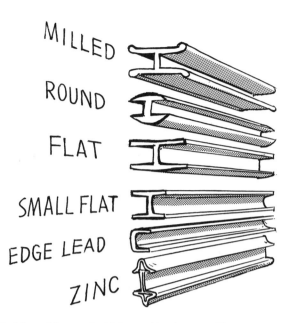

4-6. A few of the most widely used lead cames. There are hundreds of different varieties manufactured.

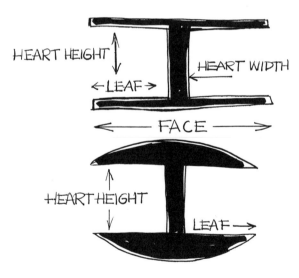

4-7. The anatomy of typical flat and round lead cames.

Solder. In most stained glass work, the solder used is called "60-40," which denotes a proportion of 60 percent tin and 40 percent lead. It comes wound on a spool, is 1/8 inch thick, and is in solid form, rather than "core." The well-known "acid core" solder should not be used for stained glass work. For smaller panels the 50-50 solder is perfectly adequate, but for larger panels that will be subjected to wind and weather, the 60-40 solder provides slightly stronger construction.

Flux. To make firm, smooth lead joints a flux must be used with the solder; the best is oleic acid liquid flux. The flux, which is applied with an inexpensive 1/2-inch brush to the juncture of the leads, causes the solder to flow to all parts of the joint. Without flux the solder will not fuse with the lead; it will roll off in drips instead.

Putty. This is also called "glazing compound." Putty makes a final bond between the glass pieces and the lead channels and prevents the panes from rattling. It also adds strength and neatness, as well as waterproofing, to the finished panels. Putty can be bought in a gray color, or a dash of mortar black can be added to tone the white putty.

Whiting (Calcium carbonate). This fine white powder is used as a final cleaning agent for stained glass work. It is sprinkled over the panel and scrubbed briskly with a stiff brush. It absorbs excess oils and gum residue, leaving a clean, sparkling surface to glass and lead.

PREPARING THE WORK AREA

The amount of room and storage space needed for leaded glass work is considerably less than that required for faceted slab glass. The work table for leaded glass need not be a very heavy one, but it should be solidly constructed so that it cannot easily be knocked off balance. Laying plywood sheets on a sawhorse is not recommended since the accidental kicking of one of the supports can have tragic results. Also, the work table for leaded glass should be made quite a bit higher than the average "sit down" table so that you are not uncomfortably hunched over your work. Stained glass work seems to be most easily accomplished when you can walk around the work and get at it from all angles.

Instead of several drawers in the table or a special cabinet for tools and supplies, consider using a couple of lightweight, shallow wood boxes; these can be easily moved around and kept conveniently within arm's reach. (You might call them "mobile drawers.")

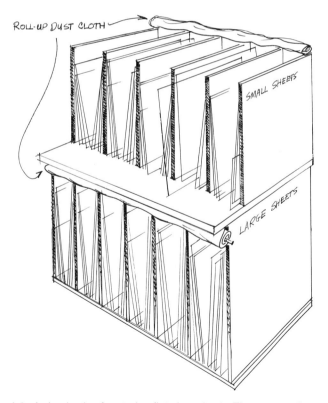

ROLL-UP DUST CLOTH

SMALL SHEETS

LARGE SHEETS

4-8. A simple plan for storing flat glass sheets. The open top is convenient for getting at smaller sheets of glass.

Aside from a simple storage rack for glass, as suggested in the illustration, there is nothing else that is essential. On second thought, there is. Working barefooted in a stained glass studio is considered courageous (although gauche), but there is another item of clothing—an apron—that is of great use, and not for reasons of modesty or safety either. The apron is frequently used to cushion the grozing pliers during the glass cutting operation.

The preceding description of tools, materials, and the work area are intended only as a minimum guide to getting started in stained glass. Further elaborations in terms of equipment, lighting, storage systems, and so forth will naturally depend on your own needs and ambitions, not to mention your budget.

DEVELOPING THE DESIGN

Whether you are an advanced art student or a rank beginner, a sense of the "structure" of lead lines in your design must be considered. In other words, the lead lines will serve a functional, as well as artistic, purpose. In good stained glass work there seems to be a happy combination of engineering and aesthetics. To illustrate, a design with many lead lines intersecting at one point makes for a weak and sloppy joint and creates an uncompromising point of focus. For another example, a design incorporating many long vertical or horizontal lead lines would leave the lead strips structurally weak, as well as create a visual dullness.

If you are about to make your first leaded glass piece, it is advisable to keep it rather simple, uncomplicated, and not too large; 1 square foot or approximately 12 by 16 inches (30 by 40 cm) is a good beginning.

It is far more interesting and challenging to invent your own design than it is to copy one of the stereotyped stained glass patterns we see so much of. A good way to develop a sketch is to make many small "doodles." Try some straight lines and some curved lines and try to get some variety in the areas of glass—large, medium, and small areas. Avoid complicated shapes. If you make about six of these small doodles on a scratch pad and then look at them from more than an arm's length away, one of them is bound to look "right." In a freehand manner, enlarge this particular one into a slightly larger, scaled sketch, first with a light pencil line and then

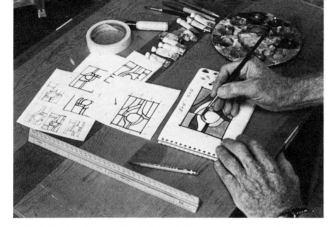

4-9. A design for your first stained glass piece evolves from several small doodles to a scaled sketch. Watercolors or pastels are used to plan the color arrangement.

4-10. Enlarge your sketch to the full-size drawing (cartoon) by sketching in the lines with a pencil and then going over them with a broad felt marker. Two copies of the cartoon are made using carbon tracing paper.

4-11. With cartoon on top, wrapping paper in the middle, and heavier kraft paper on the bottom, a pencil tracing is made. A single line drawn down the middle of the heavy cartoon lines will make both the working drawing and the cutting pattern.

firming up the lines with a black felt marker or india ink. (See instructions for enlarging designs under "Making the Cartoon" in Chapter 3.) Color in the various areas with crayon or watercolors, according to the colors of glass you have on hand.

MAKING THE CARTOON

The next step is to redraw this sketch to the larger working size. Use your drafting instruments—T square and triangle—so that all corners are squared up. In free hand, lightly sketch the various areas of your design. When these look right, heavy-up the lines to approximate the width of your leads. For variation, you may wish to use some of the wider 3/8-inch lines along with your 1/4-inch lines; for the outside borders use the stronger 3/8-inch leads. You needn't color in the cartoon unless at this stage you wish to try a different color combination.

MAKING THE PATTERN

You will need two copies of the cartoon; one will be used for placing on the work surface, the other will be cut up into template guides. Both of these can be made simultaneously with the use of carbon tracing paper. First, slip a sheet of paper (about the weight of wrapping paper) under your cartoon. Second, slip a sheet of heavier kraft paper (about the thickness of a manila folder) under the wrapping paper. Place your carbon paper facedown between these sheets. Secure this whole assembly of paper with thumbtacks or tape, so that they cannot shift around and disturb the exact "register" of your tracing operation. It is a good idea to code the various areas of your design with numbers or a color notation for later assembly. Using a hard pencil, trace down the *center* of your heavy lead lines; you need only *one* line to follow when cutting your pattern and assembling the glass and lead.

CUTTING THE PATTERN

The bottom sheet of heavier kraft paper is now ready to be cut into separate pieces. For this you will need either the double-cutting pattern shears or either of the substitute devices described under "Tools." The thin filigree of paper that you cut from between the areas of your pattern represents the "heart" of the lead cames. This amount of space *must* be allowed for; otherwise, your panel won't fit together properly. Cut one area at a time, always cutting a little beyond the junction of the lines, so that when you start the cut for the adjoining pieces you will have an *exact* starting position. It is useful, though not

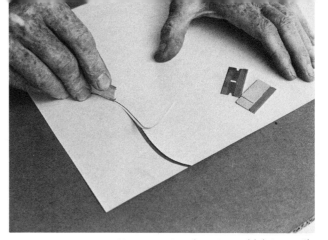

4-14. Cardboard provides a good surface over which to use the double-edged razor blade when cutting the pattern.

4-12. Using a straightedge and razor, the edges of the cutting pattern are trimmed to the "cut line" size.

4-13. An inexpensive substitute for the pattern shears is made from two single-edged razor blades taped together.

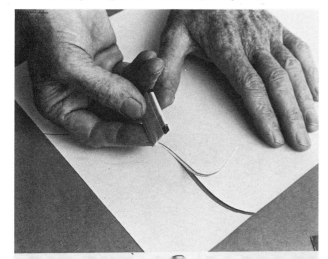

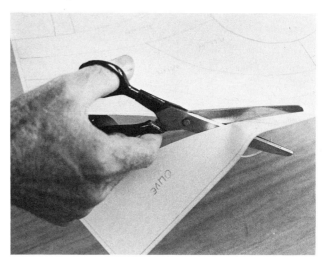

4-15. Paper and pattern shears are manipulated in the hands when cutting the curved lines of the design.

4-16. The pattern shears, made especially for stained glass work, accurately cut out a 1/16-inch strip of paper from between adjoining areas of the pattern. The glass pieces will not fit together unless you remove this thin strip.

essential, to spray some adhesive or lightly coat the *back* of your cutting pattern with rubber cement; this way, the pattern pieces will not slip around on the glass surface when you use the glass cutter.

CUTTING THE GLASS

Each separate piece you have cut from your paper pattern is now used as a template or guide for cutting corresponding glass pieces. If you are inexperienced with the glass cutter, a good procedure is to get some (free) scraps of ordinary window glass from your local dealer and spend some time practicing a variety of cuts. (Ask for "double-strength" glass; that is, 1/8- [3mm] inch-thick window glass.)

For cutting straight lines, lay a ruler or straightedge on the glass, holding it steadily in position; with the other hand, make a steady pass with the glass cutter, pressing steadily, but rather lightly. Try to maintain an *even* pressure from beginning to end, and let your whole arm, rather than wrist or fingers, do the work. Don't bear down and *never* go back over the cut, since this damages the cutting wheel. Gently tap the glass from the end; it should break cleanly along the line.

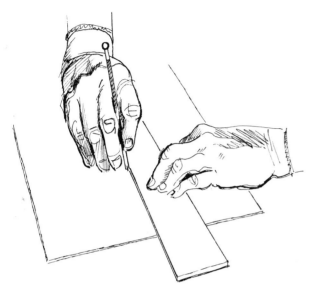

4-17a. When using the straightedge very little *lateral* pressure is needed to guide the cutter; a bit more pressure is put *downward* on the cutter.

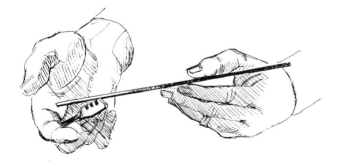

4-17b. When tapping underneath the scored line, never use the wheel.

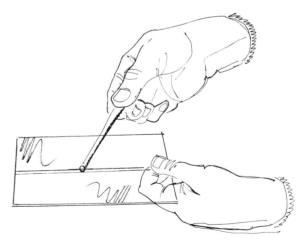

4-18. The glass is tapped directly under the scored line.

For cutting larger freehand curves, follow the same procedure; for smaller curves of a shorter radius, it is necessary to accomplish this in several cuts, removing each small section with the grozer until you reach the innermost line. For cutting complete circles, there is a circle-cutting attachment that one can purchase. A carefully made template can also be used for cutting circles of a larger diameter.

The hardness and tensions of different types of glass can vary considerably and react individually to the cutter, but with a certain amount of repeated practice you will inevitably develop the touch for the glass cutter.

The paper pattern piece can be placed or taped under the glass. For economy's sake, cut a larger piece of glass from a corner or end of the stained glass sheet, leaving about 1/2 inch (12mm) of space around your pattern. Snap off this piece before beginning your precise pattern cut. Guide the glass cutting wheel along the edge of your paper pattern and snap off each cut as it is made. Extreme precision is not absolutely necessary in cutting the pattern pieces, since there is a certain flexibility of fit in putting the panel together. However, it is best to make the cuts as carefully as you can; the more accurate the cut, the less problems when assembling the panel. As you cut each piece of glass, it is a good idea to dull the sharp edges with emery paper or a file; not only will the further handling of the glass be much safer, but the fit into the lead channels will be better.

4-19. The usual method of holding the glass cutter.

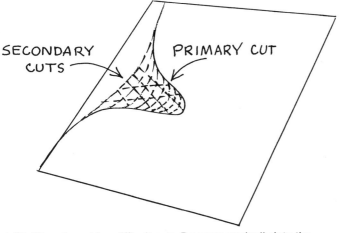

SECONDARY CUTS

PRIMARY CUT

4-20. Steps in making difficult cuts. Progress gradually into the curve, grozing away small bits of glass at a time.

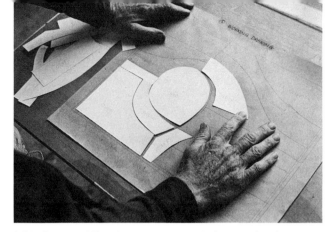

4-21. Reassembling the cut-up pattern before cutting the individual glass pieces.

4-24. The trick to cutting glass with the straightedge is to keep it from sliding. Use a gentle pressure against the straightedge while applying more pressure downward.

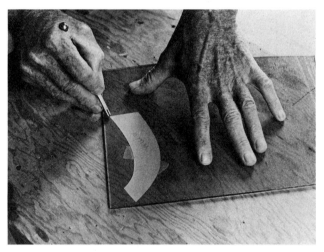

4-22. When cutting curved pieces, the template can be held firmly in place on top of the glass or taped underneath the glass.

4-25. An alternate method of separating glass in straight cuts is to lay the cut-line on the edge of a wood strip and press downward with a rapid motion of the thumb.

4-26. Where a curve meets a straight line, continue the curve *past* the corner, gradually easing to the edge of the glass. Separate the entire shape from the glass sheet before snapping off the smaller piece to form the square corner.

4-23. While one hand taps the cut-line, the other hand straddles both sides of the line to prevent the cut piece from falling.

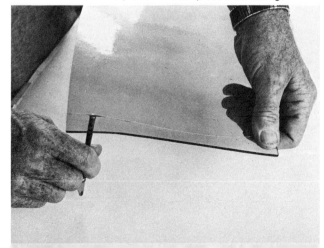

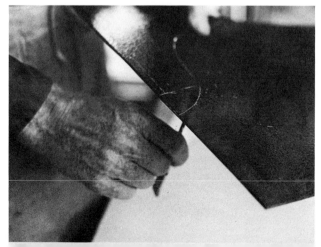

4-27. For snapping off long, thin strips, cushion the jaws of the grozing pliers in the work apron; there is less chance of cracking the glass or chipping the edges this way.

PREPARING THE WORK SURFACE

Lay the line tracing of your design (the wrapping paper sheet) out on the work board, square it up, and tape it in place. Cut two strips of wood lath. These are available at the lumberyard in long lengths; 1/4 inch thick (7mm) by 1 inch wide (25mm) is a convenient size to work with. Using short nails, secure a lath strip along one entire side of the drawing. Nail another strip along the bottom of the drawing, so that you have formed a tight, wooden, 90-degree corner. If you are using the 3/8-inch leads as an outside border, note that your "cut line" or glass line should be about 3/16 inch (4mm) *inside* the borders of your drawing.

4-28. When cutting odd-shaped pieces of glass it is important to tap accurately along the entire cut-line from below.

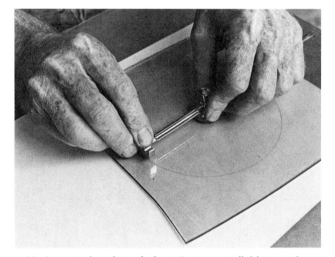

4-30. Inexpensive glass circle-cutters are available to make accurate circle cuts. They can be adjusted for various sizes.

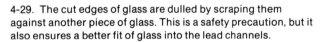

4-29. The cut edges of glass are dulled by scraping them against another piece of glass. This is a safety precaution, but it also ensures a better fit of glass into the lead channels.

4-31. The working drawing is taped to the work surface. Wood strips are nailed into place, forming a right angle along the bottom and one side.

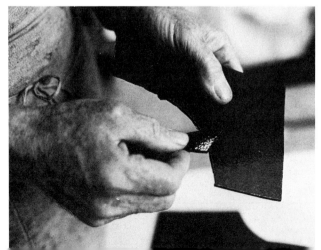

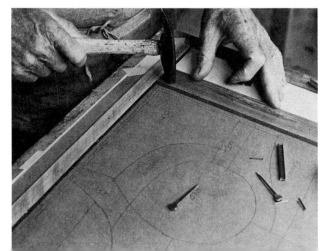

ASSEMBLING THE LEAD AND GLASS

You start the assembly with two pieces of 3/8-inch lead; one runs up the side of your design, the other runs across the bottom. Measure and cut off enough lead to fit both the side and bottom border, leaving a slight extra allowance. You will then stretch the lead by locking one end (about 1/2 inch) into the vise, getting a good grasp on the other end of the lead with the pliers, and pulling. Before pulling the lead, however, straighten out any twists or kinks and make sure that the channel of the lead is aligned in the direction of your pull. When stretching lead, brace yourself well and then pull, *gradually* and steadily. As a rule of thumb, lead can be stretched

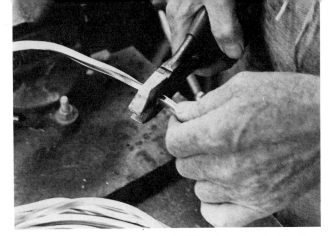

4-34. Before stretching leads, cut off the size needed with pliers or scissors.

4-32. Two border leads are placed against the wood and held in place with nails.

4-33. Lead is soft and easily kinked and twisted out of shape. Before using, it must first be stretched and straightened out. Leads that are 1/4 inch and smaller can be rolled, but 3/8-inch or larger leads should be kept in 6-foot flat lengths.

4-35. About 1/2 inch of lead is clamped into the vise. Any size bench vise will do or, lacking this, an inexpensive lead vise is recommended.

4-36. When stretching leads first get rid of twists, aligning the flanges in the direction of your pull. Pull gradually; don't yank.

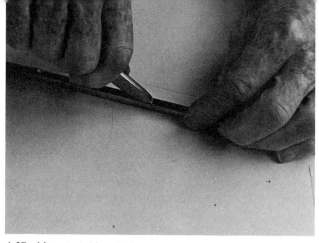

4-37. After stretching the leads, open up the length of the channel with the lathekin or handle of a table knife.

4-38. When cutting lead, rock the knife slightly while applying a gradual downward pressure.

4-39. The channel of the border lead is opened up to accept the adjoining piece easily. After inserting the adjoining lead, tap the joint lightly to flatten it out.

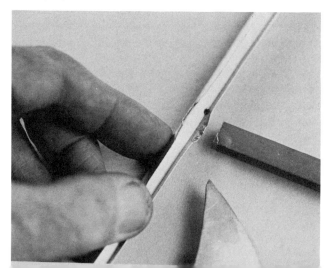

1/2 to 1 inch for every foot of length; lead does vary in its consistency and will probably break, at either the plier or the vise end before it can be stretched too far.

After it has been stretched, you will find that the lead came is quite taut and structurally stronger than it was in its previous limp state. All of the leads that go into your panel must, of course, be stretched even though they may eventually be used in curved lines or in circles. After stretching, lay the lead pieces on the flat surface and run the lathekin down the channels, opening them evenly, but not excessively, so that they will eventually receive the glass pieces easily. (A drop of liquid flux on the lathekin will help it slide easily down the channel; don't use oil, since it would retard later soldering.) Make a clean cut on one end of the lead and fit the cut end into the corner of your wood lath guides. Cut the other lead to join or butt against it, forming a tight lead corner. These border leads can extend a little beyond the top and side of your design; they will be trimmed off later. You will notice that the cutting of the leads goes easier when you *rock* the knife while gradually pressing down; it is not a sawing or slicing motion. Inevitably, some of the cuts will tend to squash the lead a bit out of shape; when this happens, pry the flanges open before placing the lead into position. The secret of cutting leads seems to be in the sharpness of the blade and the evenness of the pressure exerted.

When joining leads, fit one lead slightly into the other by opening up the channel; some artists like to sandpaper or shave the surface of one lead with a razor to make a very neat fit and strong joint.

You are now ready to fit the first piece of glass into the corner junction; it must be fitted *into* the channels. With a small block of wood, tap it in lightly for a good fit. Naturally, you should never tap the glass with the hammer, since it will chip or shatter it. Measure your next lead came by laying it alongside the glass piece already in place, marking off the length on the lead with a knife or pencil. Cut it to size and fit it back into position, again tapping lightly with the flat wood block. Proceed in this manner to fit glass and cut leads, working from one corner in a diagonal direction across your design; this way you are always working from a firm corner. There is no reason why you can't work from bottom to top, or left to right, providing that you don't box yourself in.

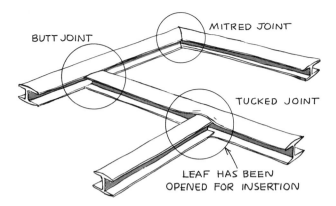

BUTT JOINT MITRED JOINT

TUCKED JOINT

LEAF HAS BEEN
OPENED FOR INSERTION

4-40. Three basic types of lead came joints. The tucked joint is the strongest; sometimes the inserted lead is shaved down for a better fit.

4-41. The first glass piece is fitted into the corner leads.

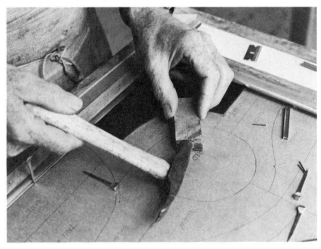

4-42. A wood block is used to tap the glass firmly into place.

4-43. Fitting the lead around a curved piece of glass.

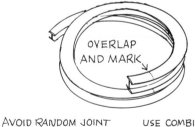

WHEN CUTTING CIRCULAR FORMS IN LEAD—

OVERLAP
AND MARK

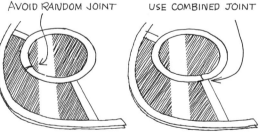

AVOID RANDOM JOINT   USE COMBINED JOINT

4-44. Cutting and fitting lead for a circular piece of glass.

55

After you have fitted a few pieces, you will find it is necessary to lightly tap a few nails into the work at strategic points so that you maintain a slight, but steady, pressure toward your starting corner. This way, as the construction grows, your carefully positioned pieces of glass will not shift around or change from your original pattern. Throughout the course of your work, if you find that a particular piece of glass is a bad fit, it is best to recut it, rather than to continue on, compounding the distortion further. As you reach the other side, or top, of your design, let the leads overlap the border line slightly; these will all be trimmed off at one operation. When you have marked, fit, and cut your two final border leads, they should be braced with two more lath strips, which are tapped firmly into position and then nailed into the work board.

As a final step before soldering the joints, be sure that they are smooth and flat. This is done by flattening them carefully with the hammer. If any of the lead joints have been cut too short or if there are small spaces between lead and glass, this is the time to repair them. Cut small strips or slivers from scrap lead and fit them into place; they will not be noticed when soldered.

4-45. Starting from one corner, the entire assemblage of glass and leads is held together with nails; a slight pressure should be maintained toward the corner throughout the assembling of the panel.

SOLDERING

The working tip of the soldering iron is not really iron; it is copper, which is a far more efficient conductor of heat. (It has retained the name from its ancient form, which was originally a heated iron.) You should make a small stand or rest for the soldering iron to keep the hot point from burning your work surface when you set it aside. An aid to maintaining an even level of heat is an off-on switch, installed about 12 to 15 inches (31 to 38cm) from the handle. (A rheostat automatic control unit is recommended if it fits into your budget.)

Before you use the new soldering iron (or the soldering gun), its tip must first be "tinned." Clean the entire copper tip with a *fine* file or emery paper, until it is a shiny copper pink, free from pits and bumps. Try not to round off the original planes of the tip. Brush the liquid solder flux (oleic acid) over the tip and then let the iron heat up. Touch the solder to the tip, and, when it begins to run, coat the entire copper tip with solder; a thin coating of solder is sufficient. A handy device for tinning, which must be done from time to time in the soldering process, is a shallow tin lid fixed to a block of wood. A generous amount of solder and flux is melted in the tin lid and the heated soldering iron is coated with flux and rubbed into the mixture. (Some artisans sprinkle a bit of rosin into the tinning lid to facilitate the tinning process.) The trick in tinning is to keep the soldering iron at just the right temperature so that the solder flows in an even coat.

As you begin the soldering operation on your panel, there are three points to remember:
1. If the solder won't flow, the iron is too cool.
2. If the solder iron melts the lead came, the iron is too hot.
3. If the solder runs off in small lumps, you forgot to apply the flux.

It is good practice to clean the lead joints before soldering them by using a small, fine wire brush, such as those used for brushing suede. Steel wool or sandpaper can also be used for this, but the suede brush is well-suited for the job.

With a small brush, apply a generous amount of flux to all the joints of the panel. Unroll about 5 inches (13cm), from the solder coil, but don't cut it off; hold the coil in one hand and unroll it gradually, as needed. Bring the solder wire and the soldering iron together, just as you touch the lead came, and flow a small amount of solder across the joint. You needn't put pressure on the lead came; the solder should flow on freely. A little preparatory practice with some lead scraps will soon give you the touch. One flowing-on of the solder will make a strong joint; you needn't pile the solder up or go over it several times. Tin melts at a lower temperature than lead; the easiest, or lowest, melting point of all tin/lead solder combinations (known as the "eutectic") is approximately 361 degrees Fahrenheit (183 degrees Centigrade). It comprises approximately 62 percent tin and 38 percent lead.

When doing the soldering, since you needn't look directly down on the soldering iron and you should try to avoid inhaling the soldering fumes, stand a bit to the side; your viewpoint will be more of a lateral one.

This is another advantage to using the "stand-up height" work table already described. In addition, the use of a fan set some distance away from the work table will deflect the soldering fumes away from you.

This safety precaution needs strong emphasis. It is only in very recent years that much attention has been paid to determining exactly how toxic the fumes from soldering are. Some people who have worked for a lifetime with the process scoff at the idea that it may have any harmful effects. While exact documentation of the subject does not seem to be available, there are definite warnings to be

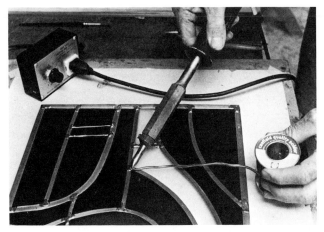

4-46. Oleic acid is applied to all joints and the entire panel is soldered. Complete one side at a time. Rheostat control maintains even heat, but an off-on switch near the soldering iron handle can also be used.

heeded; it appears that individual sensivity to poisoning from lead soldering varies greatly, and some cases of illness, however uncommon they may appear to be, have been reported.

There is a growing and very sensible awareness of such potential hazards in all of the arts and the crafts. Today, the message is clear; it is better to pay attention to the proverbial "ounce of prevention" than to pay the consequences.

Once all the joints have been soldered, wipe off any excess flux on the panel while checking to see that all joints have been completed. When one side of the panel has been soldered, the other side must be done. First, remove the wood lath strips that are holding the panel in place. You will not need these anymore, since the soldering on one side is enough to hold the panel together. Take care in turning the panel over; it is still in a fragile condition and lifting up from one end could cause it to buckle. A safe method is to first slide the panel so that it aligns with the edge of the work board; lay a piece of plywood of about the same size on top of the panel so that you have a sandwich of wood, stained glass panel, and wood. Then, keeping the flush ends on the work table, turn the whole affair over carefully and remove the work board. There are other ways of turning the panel over that involve projecting it over the edge of your work table, but care must be taken to support it at both ends, as well as at the middle, *simultaneously,* in the turning process.

Before you begin to solder the second side, you should check to see that all leads are straight and that none have been bent out of shape during the process of glass fitting. All the joints should again be inspected for fit and flattened out by tapping with the hammer. Any gaps in the joints should be filled in with small scraps of lead. You can then proceed to solder the second side, remembering to apply flux to all the joints.

PUTTYING AND CLEANING

With a blob of putty in your hand, use your thumb to work the putty under the leads, as well as all the corners of the joints. Complete one glass area at a time. When all areas have been puttied, use the lathekin along the flanges of the lead, exerting enough pressure to press them flat against the glass; this squeezes out the excess putty and makes most of it stay under the lead where it should be. You gather the excess putty up into a ball as you go along. Sliding a sharpened round stick, about the size of a pencil, along the flanges of the leads will effectively clean the edges and corners of the joints. It is best to use a wood stick, rather than a metal tool for this; the metal could scratch the glass or slip out of your hand and crack the glass.

Before turning over the panel to putty the other side, wipe the entire surface lightly with a touch of mineral spirits on a rag. Be somewhat sparing with the mineral spirits, since too much can thin out your putty. Turn the panel over and repeat the puttying operation.

A final cleaning should be given to both sides of the panel. Start by sprinkling a handful of whiting over all areas of the panel. Then, using a clean household scrub brush, scrub the entire panel then poured liberally over the panel, and a stiff scrub powder off the panel and repeat the operation on the other side. If there has been an excess of putty used in the puttying operation, you may have to give the panel a second rubbing over with the whiting. For the second cleaning, if it is necessary, use another clean brush that has been especially reserved for that purpose. This should result in a sparkling, clean surface of both glass and leads.

Any excess putty remaining should be put back into the putty container and protected from the air with some plastic film; putty exposed to air soon becomes hard and cannot be used.

There is an alternate method of puttying panels which some artists use. It has the one advantage of being a faster operation, but there are two disadvantages. For one thing, it creates a considerable mess in the studio with consequently longer cleaning-up time needed. Secondly, the panels must be stored for a longer period of time before they can be handled or installed. In this method, however, steel sash putty is diluted with a mixture of linseed oil and turpentine to the consistency of heavy cream. It is

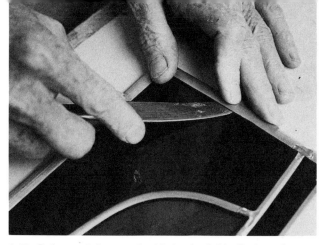

4-47. Before puttying, run the blade of a dull knife down the lead flanges to ensure sufficient space for putty.

4-48. The putty is squeezed into place between lead and glass. A rubber glove finger protects your fingers from getting cut on the lead flange.

4-49. The lathekin or a shaped hardwood stick is run down the edges of the leads to flatten out the flanges.

4-50. Excess putty is removed by running a pointed stick along the lead flanges.

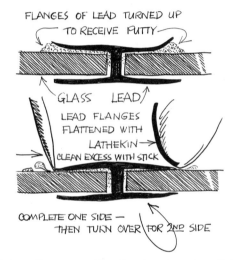

FLANGES OF LEAD TURNED UP
TO RECEIVE PUTTY

GLASS   LEAD

LEAD FLANGES
FLATTENED WITH
LATHEKIN

CLEAN EXCESS WITH STICK

COMPLETE ONE SIDE —
THEN TURN OVER FOR 2ND SIDE

4-51. Schematic cross section showing stages in puttying a panel.

4-52. After puttying, the panel is cleaned. Whiting (calcium carbonate) is sprinkled over the panel and then wiped off with a rag.

then poured liberally over the panel, and a stiff scrub brush is used to work the putty under the leads and into all joints. After this, the edges of the lead flanges are crimped flat with the lathekin. To clean off the excess putty, sawdust is sprinkled generously over the panel and the entire surface is scrubbed vigorously with a rag. (The sawdust blots up the oil of the putty.) The remaining sawdust is brushed away from the panel and the panel is given another scrubbing with a clean scrub brush and the whiting powder as described above. The operation, of course, must be repeated on the other side of the panel. When this method of a thinner consistency of putty is used, you must wait a considerably longer period of time for the panels to set up before you handle or install them.

4-53. Excess whiting is removed and glass and leads are brightened by scrubbing with a household brush.

It is recommended that for about the first 6 months of their life exterior stained glass panels should not be anything more than lightly dusted off with a brush or very lightly passed over with a dampish cloth. The seal between glass and putty might be disturbed, otherwise, and could cause the panel to leak during heavy rains. The lead cames of an interior panel can be brightened up, if desired, by a *light* rubbing with fine steel wool.

It should be noted that the preceding description of the making of a stained glass panel is essentially an outline or basic guide. The possibilities for innovation and invention from an artistic, as well as a technical, point of view are practically limitless; but new departures generally start from a well-grounded control of the craft.

ADDITIONAL USEFUL EQUIPMENT

A "light table" or a light box can be very helpful in stained glass work; with it you can arrange your individual cut glass pieces, giving you a good advance comparison of color relationships and values before you assemble your panel. The advantage of the light box versus the light table is that it can be placed on any convenient surface and stored out of the way when not needed. Space permitting, however, you might prefer the light table, which can be built as large and as high as you wish.

The light table can be made of standard 3/4-inch (18mm) lumber or plywood. It should be sufficiently deep—let's say 12 to 15 inches (30 to 38mm)—and should accommodate several fluorescent (rather than incandescent) light fixtures in its base. (Specify "cool-white" lamps since these seem to have less color distortion than others.) The top edges of the light box are rabbeted to take a flush fit of 1/4-inch (7mm) plate glass that is "frosted" on one side. If the glass supplier does not have the frosted glass in stock, take the glass to the nearest monument service for a light sandblasting of one side. Place the smooth, unfrosted side up. A coat of white paint on the interior of the box, before installing the light fixtures, will increase the illumination. One can also line the inside of the box with shiny aluminum foil. Don't forget a sufficiently long electric cord and a line switch that is convenient to the work area. The overall size is a matter of preference; a light box

4-54. The finished panel set into an outside window.

approximately 20 by 30 inches (50 by 76mm) provides a generous working area and is still not too cumbersome to be moved around.

There is another means of "pre-viewing" stained glass work which allows you to see it in its eventual intended condition. In other words you can see it, standing upright, against daylight, and with the lead lines duplicated, which, of course, can never be done with a light table.

This method requires that you lay plate glass on top of the cut-line tracing, which is put face down (or reversed) on a table. You then clean the surface of the plate glass. Paint along the cut lines, approximating the width of your lead cames, with a brush and a mixture of lamp black, a bit of gum arabic, plus, of course, a little water to make it flow. Put a heavy black border around the edges of the panel or fix on a black paper mask with a touch of rubber cement. When this has dried, turn the plate glass panel over and, at every juncture of the lead lines, press on a small ball of about 1/2 inch (12mm) of Plasticine clay. You can now position each piece of your cut glass shapes, pressing firmly into the clay lumps. The whole assembly can then be safely handled and positioned upright against daylight. Naturally, the upright panel should not be exposed to direct sunlight for more than a very short time for fear of softening the clay lumps and the consequent slipping of some of the small panes. Viewing the panels against northern light will avoid this problem. As an added precaution, lay the panels flat if they have to be stored overnight. It is evident that there is a considerable amount of additional time and work involved in this method, but for critical or large-scale commission, it is well worth the effort.

PAINTED AND FIRED GLASS

Stained glass can be fired for many smaller-sized windows and craft projects (such as wall hangings, wind chimes, and fused glass), with an electric enameling kiln or an electric ceramic kiln. These kilns are relatively inexpensive. Due to the size limitations of these small kilns, however, not to mention the much greater degree of control needed, the larger and more expensive glass kilns must be used when extensive firing is needed for stained glass windows.

Glass painting and firing is a fairly complex procedure, which really deserves a separate volume as guidance in the various techniques. (See the Bibliography.) It is recommended that the beginning student of stained glass try to establish a working arrangement with a stained glass studio that has a glass firing kiln. The studio may be able to sell you the necessary paints and brushes with, perhaps, some basic instructions, as well. This way you can at least become acquainted with the process before deciding to invest in the fairly expensive equipment (mainly the kiln) that will be necessary.

The painting and firing of stained glass has always been an integral part of the craft. If you have ever studied the magnificent early Gothic stained glass windows, you will have noticed that they are composed of more than a pattern of colored pieces of glass set in a matrix of lead cames; the individual pieces in the pattern have been painted in detail and fired in a kiln. For example, the head of a figure may be *one* piece of glass (of an amber or ochre tone), surrounded and joined to its neighbors by the lead cames. However, the *features* of the head—eyes, nose, mouth, and so forth—have been painted on the glass, which was then fired in a high-temperature kiln so that the paint *fused* with the glass surface and became a permanent part of its structure. After it was painted and fired, it was assembled into the total design. The wonderful impact of these early Gothic windows lies undoubtedly in the compatible combination of bold, mosaiclike patterns of strong color areas in harmony with the stylistic, often naive, directness of the painting.

During the later age of the Renaissance, painters were concerned with light and shade, depth of field, and "naturalism," but these concerns were never happily translated into the art of stained glass. This,

along with a number of other influences, brought about a subsequent decline in the vitality of the stained glass art.

A great deal of painted and fired glass is being done today; a large proportion of it, however, is turned out by long-established commercial firms and has a decidedly archaic, conventional look to it. The few windows that have been done by such modern masters as Matisse, Léger, Rouault, Braque, and Chagall stand out as pioneering exceptions to the rule.

In very recent years there has been a veritable profusion of new directions in stained glass; the influence of the concepts of modern painting and sculpture is much in evidence. One characteristic of modern glass work is a lesser emphasis on the painted image in glass, and more of an emphasis on the pure use of glass as a color area, which is similar to the "color field" direction of abstract painting.

COPPER FOIL
The copper foil process is used almost exclusively for making lampshades and various stained glass craft products of a smaller and more delicate nature. The thin copper is available in either sheets or in rolls of narrow tape. The most commonly used tape is the adhesive-backed narrow strip that is unwound from a roll and crimped along the edges of the glass pieces. When two pieces of glass are to be joined, the copper is brushed with flux and the solder is run along the adjoining copper surfaces, bonding them together. In this way, curved surfaces, as well as individually curved pieces of glass, can be easily managed.

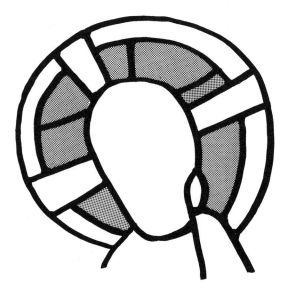

COLORED GLASS AND LEAD

COLORED GLASS & LEAD PLUS PAINTING, STAINING & FIRING

4-55. Schematic diagram showing basic stages in stained glass work. (Based on detail from a twelfth-century window, Chartres Cathedral.)

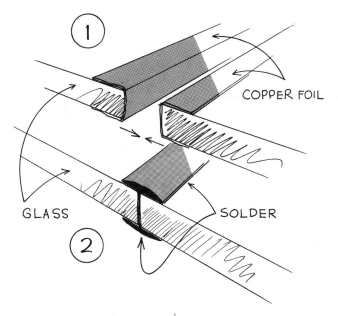

4-56. Schematic drawing showing the principle of copper foil work. First adhesive-backed copper tape is crimped around the edge of the glass. Edges of glass are joined, fluxed, and then soldered along the adjoining edges.

4-57. The austere and the lyrical are combined in Johannes Schreiter's work of 1971. Antique glass plus obscure glass in a highly disciplined matrix of leads of varying widths. (Photo by Edith Schreiter-Diedrichs)

1.

2.

3.

4.

1. When this faceted glass design was in the black-and-white cartoon stage the black line pattern was very stark. Now the line "fuses" into the color pattern due to the variations in advancing and receding colors and the use of full value scale in the design.

2. A laminated glass space divider in a commercial building in Colorado Springs, Colorado.

3. California artist Judy Jansen created unusual undulating optical surfaces by incorporating dimensional hand-blown glass shapes into her leaded glass work. (Courtesy of the artist)

4. *Colorado Landscape.* A leaded glass design in antique glass with small insets of faceted glass.

5.

6.

7.

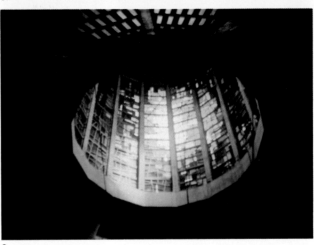

8.

5. Circular faceted glass window showing the use of broken color to avoid the feeling of symmetry usually adopted in circular forms.

6. Laminated glass clerestory in the United States Air Force Chapel in Colorado Springs, Colorado.

7. Large belfry tower window done in laminated glass. At night this window is effectively lit by floodlights on the planking of the roof structure.

8. This massive faceted glass-in-concrete work is seen above the altar in Liverpool's Roman Catholic Church. Created by the British artists, John Piper and Patrick Reyntiens. (Photo by the author)

9. Carved walnut door inset with stained glass for a communications company in Denver, Colorado.

10. A faceted slab glass window on the theme of "wine" done for a California vineyard. The textural character of faceted glass

strikes a natural harmony with the rugged character of the stonework. Window designed by Robert Pinart, executed by the Cummings Studio, 1974. (Courtesy of Cummings Studio)

11. This faceted church window depicts an early Christian symbol of life. The red, orange, and yellow pieces in the butterfly were mortised and joined.

12. In the Community Methodist Church of Santa Clara, California, is this remarkable example of restrained drawing directly translated into lead lines encompassing one color. The painted images are equally simplified. Designed by Don Cochran, executed by Hilda Sachs of the Cummings Studio. (Courtesy of Cummings Studio).

13. Two sides of 1/4-inch laminated plate glass work.

14. A freestanding stained glass sculpture by Robert Pinart. The technique utilizes opal and antique leaded glass set in a cast epoxy frame. (Courtesy of the artist)

9.

10.

11.

12.

13.

14.

15.

16.

17.

18.

15. Detail of a faceted glass panel showing technique of mortising and joining glass that has been cut on a lapidary saw.

16. The abstract, but gustatory, shapes of Otto Rigan's designs for a series of windows in an Atwater, California delicatessen. An interesting combination of cream-colored and clear glass, using two different widths of lead. (Courtesy of Cummings Studio)

17. Other side of welded sculpture showing insets of stained glass.

18. This detail shows the effect of the disappearance of black lines between colors that are held in strong structures of blacks.

19. Detail of a faceted glass work showing the inside curves and circular shapes possible to achieve with a lapidary saw.

20. Masonic Memorial Window in Colorado Springs, Colorado done in laminated glass showing the result of leaving some of the base glass clear.

21. A faceted glass work illustrating use of black areas to increase depth of red colors.

22. Detail of a window showing combination of laminated and faceted glass.

23. A circular tower done in faceted slab glass, designed and executed by Gabriel Loire of France for the Museum of Modern Art in Hakon, Japan. Loire's pioneering experiments with thick glass began in 1935. Of the dalles de verre, or faceted slab glass, technique Loire says, "It permits me a free expression within a medium of rugged character that is always pure and strong because faceted glass diffuses light in a unique way, transforming each piece into a jewel, and, because, above all, faceted glass harmonizes naturally with contemporary architecture."

24. Two of a dozen windows featuring traditional German crests done for a Vail, Colorado ski lodge. Intricacies of lettering and design are more easily accomplished with the laminated glass technique than with the leaded glass technique.

19.

20.

21.

22.

23.

24.

69

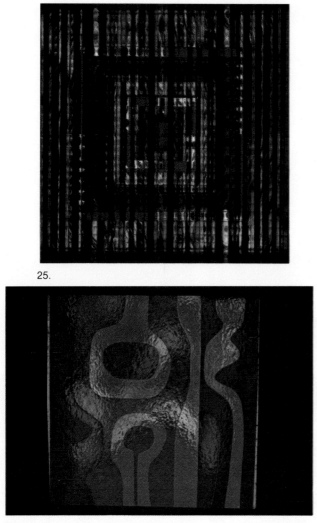

25.

26.

27.

25. One of Fredrica Field's luminous multilayered glass constructions. A variety of antique sheet glass, glass tubes, and faceted glass. The work is 30 by 30 inches and 6 inches deep and is back-lit. One of three created for the YWCA of Greenwich, Connecticut. (Photo by Kenneth Fields)

26. Acrylic sheet cut to pattern and laminated. Notice how the acrylic has a different "flow" as compared to glass.

27. Detail of a sculptured concrete wall by Don Shepard, showing textures obtained by using such things as burlap, rope, and shaped vinyl in the mold. Some of the slab glass insets were cast in the mold, while others were fit into openings after concrete was cured. (Photo by the artist)

28. An example of the precise "minimalist" work of Dick Weiss of Seattle, Washington. Glass is obscure white, black, and clear. (Courtesy of the artist)

29. Variations in straight and curved elements in this faceted glass work were made solely with the use of the lapidary saw. (From the Walsky Collection, Colorado)

30. Dalles de verre work on a heroic scale. A building totally enclosed in faceted slab glass. The precast panels were designed and executed by the master glass worker Gabriel Loire in his studios in France for the Bacardi Company building in Miami, Florida.

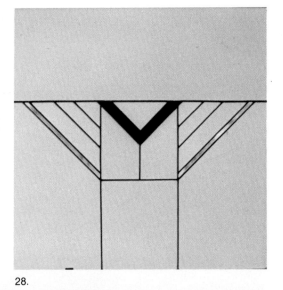

28.

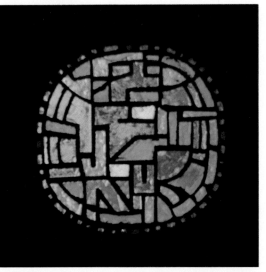

29.

30.

31.

32.

33.

34.

31. Concrete mural in Colorado Springs, Colorado featuring glass, mosaics, and mirrors cast into concrete.

32. Sculpture for a churchyard in Colorado Springs, Colorado.

33. Welded steel sculpture done for the Denver, Colorado Public Library.

34. *Airport, Colorado Springs*. This exhibition piece features four layers of laminated glass with fluorescent lighting.

→

4-58. A dynamic use of the diagonal with highly inventive leading shown in Johannes Schreiter's 1974 window. Schreiter, together with fellow Germans Wilhelm Buschulte, Georg Meistermann, and Ludwig Schaffrath, are the center of a new school of modern stained glass work that completely breaks with the tradition of representational symbolism. (Photo by Edith Schreiter-Diedrichs)

4-59. Narcissus Quagliata's *My Androgynous Shadow*; 1975, 46 by 72 inches. The stark silhouette is black obscure glass and is entrapped in a delicate web of lead lines and shimmering antique glass. Quagliata is the author of the delightful book *Stained Glass—From Mind to Light.* (Photo by the artist)

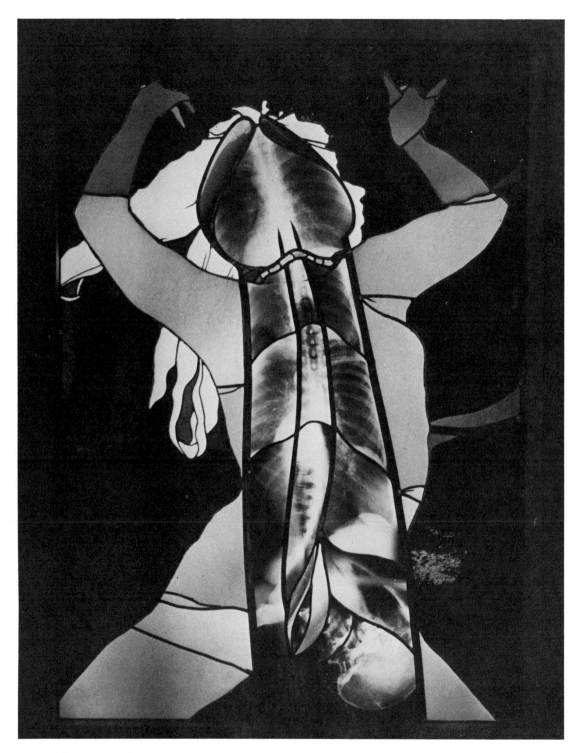

4-60. Stained glass with X-ray film laminated between clear glass. California artist Narcissus Quagliata's *Opal Dance After the Earthquake*, 1977, 42 by 60 inches. (Photo by Bill Kane)

4-61. One of Richard Posner's enigmatic stained glass windows; "His Master's Voice" (26 by 30 inches, 1975). Posner utilizes combinations of highly patterned commercial glasses plus the painted image. (Photo by Durstin Saylor)

4-62. There is fantasy and humor in Robert Kehlmann's work; it gently teases the "ancient craft" with "impossible" glass cutting and leading and a strong use of opaque glass. Kehlmann's *Composition XXIV* is 32 by 29 inches.

Kehlmann states, "The medievals taught us that successful stained glass must be essentially two-dimensional. Why then do

I build outward from the windowpane with wires and pieces of glass? The sculptural relief on my panels, in conjunction with appliqued lead lines, allow me to explore visually phenomena which cannot be explored through a more traditional use of glass and lead. I can mix textures and colors, make use of discontinuous lines, or draw forms that are impossible to cut with a glass cutter. My elevated forms redefine the shapes of the pieces of glass beneath them without denying a fundamental flatness of design. My work ultimately has a closer affinity to contemporary drawing than it does to traditional stained glass." (Photo by Charles Frizzell; Courtesy of the Jenkins-Wiley Collection, Albany, California)

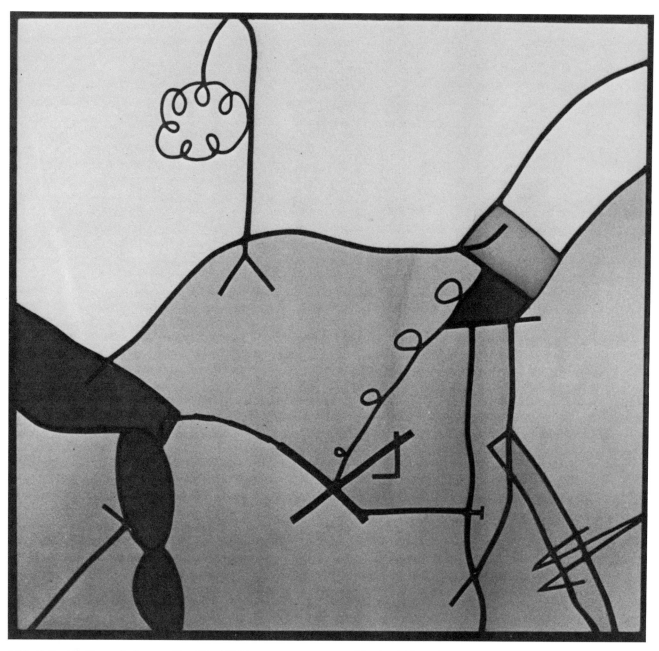

4-63. Robert Kehlmann's *Composition XXXII*. Kehlmann states, "I don't use transparent glass because I don't want people looking *through* my windows. What lies behind the compositions, aside from a source of light, has no relevance to my design. My windows are architectural only to the degree that a painting or a piece of sculpture placed inside a building is architectural. There is no reason why stained glass should have any limitations beyond those dictated by materials and a sensitivity to design." Splitting of the leads and bonding them with epoxy to the surface of the glass helps to achieve some of the improbable free-form "cutting" in Kehlmann's work. (Photo by Lee Fatherree)

4-64. Stained glass in an architectural setting by Peter Mollica
of California. A student of the contemporary masters of German
stained glass work, Mollica makes very effective use of
transparent and obscure glass. The design is a dynamic
response within an essentially static environment.

4-66. Nature is closely and lovingly observed in Kathie Bunnell's work. The lead cames emphasize the "drawing" of the design. The artist incorporates intricately leaded details with very sparing use of sandblasting. The work is called *Nasturtium (Day)*, 1976, 17 1/4 by 24 inches. (Photo by the artist)

4-65. Peter Mollica's stained glass window for a bathroom. The grid lines of the tiles lead into the design of the lead cames. (Photo by Charles Frizzell)

4-67. An example of contemporary German stained glass.
Georg Meistermann's work emphasizes leading more as a
textural element than as a demarcation between color areas.
Detail from a project in Frankfurt/Main, Germany. (Courtesy of
the artist)

CHAPTER 5.

WORKING WITH LAMINATED GLASS

Laminated glass, which is generally not painted and fired, is the most direct and least complex kind of art work that can be done in glass. In terms of materials needed and technical skill required, laminated glass poses no great demands. Any type of relatively flat-coloredglass can be used to make laminated stained glass work. (See "Types of Glass".)

Basically, laminated glass consists of flat-colored glass that is cut to a pattern and then superimposed with a clear epoxy resin on a glass base. After the resin adhesive has cured, the interstices between the colored glass are filled in with a dark-colored grout. Thus, the general appearance of laminated glass is quite similar to that of leaded glass work.

One of the unique qualities of laminated glass is that the black grouted line, analogous to the cames in leaded work, can vary greatly from thin to very wide. Consequently, patterns of considerable intricacy or of very delicate scale, as well as those that call for geometric precision, can readily be accomplished. The laminated technique does not lend itself well to the "realism" of images, which painted and fired leaded glass is more naturally geared to.

With the double-lamination technique, in which colored glass is bonded to *both* sides of a clear glass base, very rich and subtle color effects can be achieved; the overlaying of one color passage through another creates the visual suggestion of an interplay of two planes.

The clear epoxy resin used for laminated glass is especially formulated for this purpose. For smaller panels, regular window glass (1/8-inch double-strength) can be used as a base for the colored glass, but for larger panels (approximately 4 square feet or larger) the strength of 1/4-inch plate glass is recommended.

CLEANING THE GLASS

A washing with a detergent solution followed by a rinsing with clean water is generally sufficient for cleaning glass. But, if the glass has any sort of paint or oily film on it, it might require razor scraping with mineral spirits, followed by detergent washing and water rinsing. It is best to avoid the widely sold all-purpose window cleaners; many of these have wax in their formulas; traces of the wax left on the surface of your glass can weaken the bond of the lamination. An excellent glass-cleaning agent is a mixture of 50 percent ammonia and 50 percent alcohol, which you can get from the druggist; this mixture, which should be cut slightly with water, should thoroughly cut any oily film or wax residue on the glass.

CUTTING THE GLASS

You are now ready to cut your pieces of colored glass and place them into position on the glass base. Avoid cutting the glass directly on your clear glass base; instead, keep a tracing of your design to one side and do all your cutting on this surface. This way, you will not scar the surface of your glass base nor will you have a lot of small scraps getting in the way. As each piece is cut, lay it into position on your glass base. When handling the glass, avoid getting fingerprints on the underside of your colored glass. The use of rubber gloves, if you don't find them bothersome to work with, will preclude this.

APPLYING THE EPOXY

When all the pieces have been cut and assembled, you will find it easier to epoxy only certain sections of your design at a time. One of the reasons for doing this is that some pieces of your assemblage may tend to slip sideways after they have been put into position. Use a small brush to apply the clear epoxy to the underside of each piece of glass. When you then put them into position, press down slightly to get rid of any air bubbles. The goal is to get a "glue line" as thin as possible and to keep air bubbles to a minimum. Thus, it helps to put some weight on the pieces you have epoxied into place. Bricks stood on their end are satisfactory, but make sure that the brick doesn't get bonded to the piece it is weighting down. For work involving small pieces of glass, use small waxed paper-cups filled with the heaviest material you can find, such as lead pellets, or even the small, round boulders found near river banks.

The aim is to bring a gradual, steady pressure to bear until the epoxy has hardened. The advantage of using the weighted cups is that the waxed paper is impervious to the epoxy. There is no danger if the cup should get stuck to the work; a razor scraper will soon free it.

One of the problems in making laminated glass panels is the trapping of air bubbles under the glass. A few small ones are not unattractive, and you might as well take credit for these. But larger air bubbles do detract from the appearance of the panel—not so much from the viewing side, where they may not even be noticed, but from the back, where they may be seen. However, there is a way to get rid of most of these air pockets. After the first application of clear epoxy has cured and the weights have been removed from the surface, a small amount of epoxy is mixed and then poured into the channels. Sometimes the panel can be tilted and the epoxy allowed to flow under the glass, a few drops at a time.

If your design goes clear to the edge of your glass base, you will want to avoid the embarassment of the excess squeezed-out epoxy having bonded your glass base to your work table. Putting a few strips of wood under the glass base to raise it up from the work surface or using some wide strips of waxed paper around and under the perimeter of your work will prevent this from happening.

Before proceeding to the next step—grouting—you can, if necessary, get rid of any excess epoxy in the channels by running a narrow screwdriver down the channel and scooping it out. This is best done when the resin has reached a heavy viscous state—approximately 8 hours after curing.

Any drops of epoxy that have fallen on the surface of your panel can be easily removed with a razor blade in a holder after curing. Brushes are cleaned with mineral spirits and washed in soap and water.

GROUTING

Allow from 12 to 18 hours for curing at room temperature before beginning the grouting.

There are a variety of materials that may be used as a grout to fill in the voids separating the glass pieces of your design. If the panels are for interior use only, there are many readily available mixtures that may be used. But if the panels are to be exposed to the weather cycle of sun, rain, and freezing

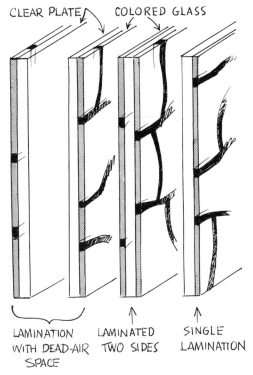

5-1. Schematic drawing of positioning of glass.

CLEAR PLATE   COLORED GLASS

LAMINATION WITH DEAD-AIR SPACE   LAMINATED TWO SIDES   SINGLE LAMINATION temperatures, *only* materials of a known standard will do.

For durability and weatherability, an epoxy grout serves the best purpose. It is impervious to water, it has good retention of mass, and it has a sympathetic coefficient of expansion and contraction with glass. An epoxy that is "drier" (in the sense that it is not thin and pourable) is easier to handle. (See "Supply List".) An addition of some fine sand will make the thinner type of epoxy more workable. The epoxy mix may be colored with mortar black—a fine, black powdered-carbon. This is used in coloring mortar and is available at paint stores or building-supply centers.

Using a broad, flexible metal spatula, mix the grout on a slab of marble, slate, or thick glass. With the spatula, force the grout into the interstices, letting it get on the surface of the glass as much as necessary. When the panel has been grouted, you now have to get rid of the excess grout that has gotten on the surface of your panel. This is done by wiping the surface with a rag and mineral spirits. The trick here is to clean the surface without dragging too much of the grout out of the interstices. Several passes with the rag over the entire panel will be necessary before the surface is suitably clean. It is best to do about 1 square foot at a time. The whole process of wiping the panels clean seems, at first try, a hopelessly messy operation. But with a little practice and the use of many rags it becomes manageable.

Easier-to-use grouts, which can only be used for panels that will not be exposed to the weather may be made in the form of a heavy paste, consisting of portland cement, a bit of mortar black, and a small amount of water. Also, such things as bath-tile grout, or black window putty, may be used. Mineral spirits is used to clean up for the tile and putty operations.

DOUBLE LAMINATION

The process of double lamination, which is the laminating of various colors of glass on both sides of the clear glass base, lends itself readily to improvisation, rather than to the strict following of a design with every detail carefully worked out in advance. The reason for this is that the overlapping colors can best be seen and experimented with as you proceed; the design is evolved in the doing. In the double-sided lamination there is inevitably a front, or primary viewing side, while the reverse side augments your original design idea.

After one side of the panel has been completed and you have turned the panel over to work on the other side, it is then advantageous to use the light box (see "Additional Useful Equipment"). With the light box you can view the whole color process as you cut, lay in each piece, and build up the pattern. When this is done and you are ready to adhere the glass pieces into place, the panel can then be carefully moved from the light box to a flat working surface.

A very interesting effect is achieved when, instead of two layers of colored glass being laminated on the front and back of a single clear panel, the two layers are made as two *separate* panels and are placed, one in front of the other, with a space of 1 inch or so separating them. Placed in a frame or casement, the phenomenon of overlapping colors is well seen. The air space adds a dimension of depth that is not achieved in any other type of stained glass. In addition, a slight change in the viewing angle gives rise to a sense of visual movement which is also quite unique to laminated glass. Aesthetics aside, architects recognize a decidedly beneficial aspect in the insulation factor of the dead-air space that is obtained in this type of fabrication.

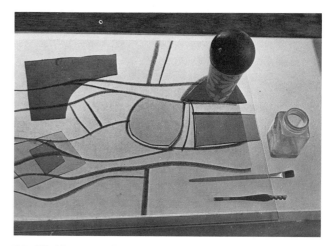

5-2. Working on the light table when making a laminated glass panel. Pieces to be laminated are best done in a "series" of one color or one section of design at a time. This will avoid excessive shifting around of glass during the time that epoxy is setting up. Steel ball (or round stones) serve to weight pieces during curing.

5-3. Fredrica Fields is noted for her multilayered glass constructions. Intriguing optical effects result from the overlaying of various types of colored flat glass, as well as glass rods and tubes. Example shown is 22 1/4 by 22 3/4 inches and stands in a Greenwich, Connecticut library. (Photo by K.E. Fields)

In a panel of a single layer of lamination, the grouted side is decidedly the primary viewing side. With its variations of different glass textures, as well as its sharply defined "black line," it presents a more attractive surface.

EXTERIOR LAMINATED PANELS

How durable are laminated panels that will be exposed out-of-doors to the weather cycle? Laminated glass panels intended for exterior use are only as durable as the epoxy resins that were used in their making. Here the artist can only rely on the manufacturer's guarantee. Another factor to be considered is the size of the panels; the larger the area of glass, the greater are the chances of excessive stress setting in as a result of solar radiation. Due to the extreme differences of climate in various parts of the country, reliable information regarding the maximum safe size of panels has not yet been compiled. Until such guidelines are available, cautious experimentation will have to suffice.

5-4. Fredrica Fields "builds" her layered glass constructions starting on a base of 1/4-inch clear glass. She designs as she builds, taking apart and putting together each layer many times before she completes the assemblage with another sheet of 1/4-inch plate held into the frame with a strip of molding. Example shown is 14 by 30 inches. (Photo by K.E. Fields)

5-5. Enlarged detail of one of Fredrica Field's multilayered glass pieces showing the shimmering luminous patterns created with the use of a wide assortment of transparent materials—antique sheet glass, rods, tubes, rondels, and faceted glass. Detail is from an exhibition panel with back-lighting. (Photo by Kenneth E. Fields)

If laminated panels are to be exposed to the weather, they should be installed with the grouted side out; much of the direct sunlight will be deflected away from the surface while some will be absorbed and transmitted in the layer of colored glass. However, if the panel is installed with the base side out, the sun's rays can come through the clear glass base without significant deflection and are absorbed at the glue line. This can create an infrared heat-ray build-up, creating internal stress sometimes sufficient to crack the panel.

Another reason for installing laminated panels with the grouted side out is that continual exposure of the epoxy glue line to ultraviolet rays can cause a milky florescence to appear after some years. The strength of the epoxy bond does not seem to be adversely affected by this however, and, as far as overall color transmission is concerned, it is a negligible factor.

It is well known that different colors of glass will expand and contract under heat according to their color value. While the clearer, lighter shades transmit more light, the darker colors absorb more light and thus retain more heat. If installed on the north side of a building or at other locations where direct sunlight does not fall, the danger of excessive heat build-up will be avoided.

5-6. This mobile light mural by Gyorgy Kepes, Professor of Visual Design at MIT, is a 51-foot-long changing pattern of lights. Located in the KLM building in New York, the design is based on "the impression a person has when flying in an airplane at night and looking down on a panorama of city lights which resembles a giant Christmas tree decorating the earth," according to Kepes. The total assemblage is made up of many aluminum panels perforated in a myriad of openings, over which thousands of pieces of colored glass were bonded with clear epoxy. The back-lighting is an intricate system of incandescent, fluorescent, and spotlights behind the mural surface that are controlled by timing and switching devices which control the pattern of light. the largest dominant panel in the mural was made by laminating colored glass to both sides of a 1/2-inch sheet of glass. (Courtesy KLM Royal Dutch Airlines)

CHAPTER 6.

INSTALLING STAINED GLASS WORK

For the reasons given in the chapter "Starting One's Own Studio," an artist should generally avoid becoming directly involved in the actual installation of art work in the building or at the site for which it was made. It is better practice to either let the client have this done directly for him at his own expense or for you to contract to have it done, adding the cost to your bill. Whatever the arrangement may be, it should be decided in the earliest possible stages of the project. In addition, you will probably have a craftsmanly, albeit parental, concern that it be done right; clear communication and any special instructions that may be necessary, should flow between yourself and the installing contractor.

In the case of stained glass, there is a difference in the way leaded, faceted, or laminated glass should be installed. But two cardinal rules apply to all three types:

1. They must be installed with sufficient clearance left so that they can expand and contract with the variations of the weather cycle.
2. They should be glazed in with a sealing agent of a permanently flexible and enduring nature.

If stained glass panels of any type are to be installed in the interior of a building or in any circumstances where they are not exposed to the weather cycle, the factor of being free-floating is, of course, not critical. They must be set into the frames snugly, so that they are free from movement. Pressure tape will suffice for interior installations.

LEADED GLASS

Leaded glass work is best fitted into durable metal frames provided with glazing beads. However, well-designed wood frames will last in direct proportion to the care with which they are maintained. Stone groove glazing must allow enough room for expansion and contraction; otherwise, there is danger of a transfer of stone movement and settling directly to leaded glass panels, which could cause stress and buckling.

Properly made leaded glass is waterproof to its edges, but for additional insulation and as protection against external damage, some leaded glass windows are being "double-glazed." Everyone seems to agree that the outside appearance of a building is hardly improved by this practice. However, when weighed against the high cost of replacing leaded glass, and when the benefits of greater temperature control are considered, double-glazing comes out the winner. Ordinary double-strength window glass is not strong enough for this purpose; 3/16- or 1/4-inch (5- or 7-mm) clear glass is sometimes used, or, if the higher impact resistance of plastics is specified by the architect, clear acrylic or polycarbonate are used. If a watertight seal is obtained in the outer "protection" pane, it is not necessary to have a watertight seal on the leaded glass. The space between outer glass and leaded glass should be a minimum of 3/4 inch (19 mm). Ideally, leaded glass panels should not exceed 16 square feet (1,486 square cm). Larger openings must have metal division bars if contiguous panels are to be set.

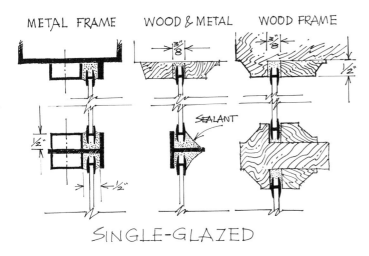

SINGLE-GLAZED

6-1. Typical details for leaded glass single-glazed.

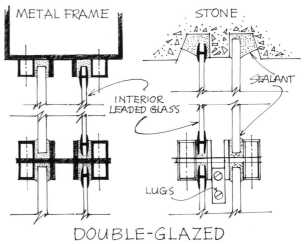

DOUBLE-GLAZED

6-2. Typical details for leaded glass double-glazed.

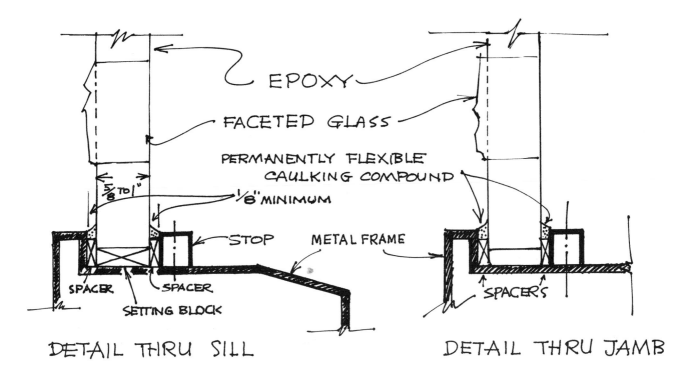

DETAIL THRU SILL

DETAIL THRU JAMB

6-3. Typical details for glazing faceted glass panels.

FACETED GLASS

Faceted glass panels can be installed in masonry, metal, or wood openings provided that frames are designed to accommodate the heavier weight (approximately 10 pounds per square foot, or 4.5 kg per 920 square cm), as well as the greater thickness of the panels. Panels should preferably be not only free-floating, but independently suspended, rather than stacked one on top of another. Because of its greater strength, faceted glass should not need to be double-glazed. Both as a bedding and a sealing bead for faceted glass panels, permanently flexible caulking, such as butyl, acrylic, silicone, or polysulfide types are recommended. Clearance of 3/16 inch (5 mm) must be allowed between frame and panel edge to allow for movement due to thermal change. Neoprene setting blocks (durometer 40–70) can be used to achieve clearance.

LAMINATED GLASS

Laminated glass panels require the same installation procedures and frames as leaded glass panels. Panels should be free-floating with allowance made for expansion and contraction. In the case of "double-glazing" with two laminated panels, install the outside pane with grouted side out and the inside pane with grouted side in; leave at least 3/4 inch (19 mm) dead-air space between panes. The maximum size for laminated panels is approximately 6 square feet (5,450 square cm) per pane.

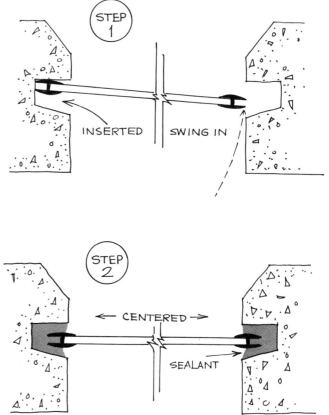

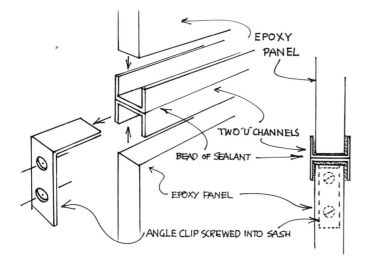

6-4. A simple horizontal divider for individual suspension of epoxy panels.

6-5. Procedure in installing leaded panels into masonry framework. Careful measurement must be taken to allow sufficient "radius" for panel to fit.

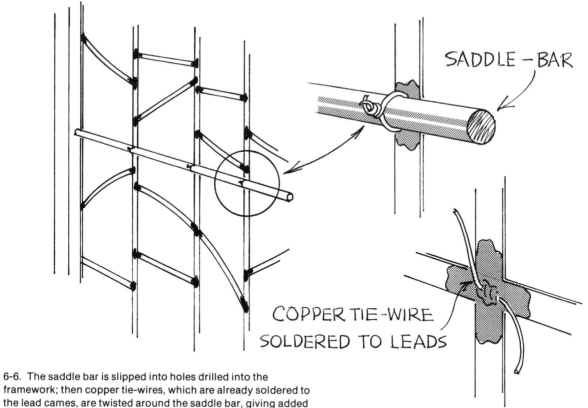

SADDLE – BAR

COPPER TIE-WIRE
SOLDERED TO LEADS

6-6. The saddle bar is slipped into holes drilled into the framework; then copper tie-wires, which are already soldered to the lead cames, are twisted around the saddle bar, giving added strength and support to the leaded window.

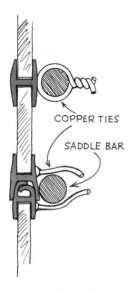

COPPER TIES

SADDLE BAR

6-7. Typical detail of method of stacking one stained glass panel on another. Copper ties from each panel secure the saddle bar at joint line.

SHIPPING STAINED GLASS WORK

If you have to ship stained glass panels, rather than delivering them yourself which is always preferable, it is important that they be packed properly. Proceed on the assumption that the crate is going to receive some rough treatment no matter how you ship it or how carefully you label it. The care in handling varies greatly from one carrier to another, whether it be by truck or by airline.

Most flat glass is shipped from factories in a flat, wood crate. The glass panes are stacked flat, one against another, in the center of the crate and cushioned by several inches of excelsior all around and at top and bottom. This method is generally acceptable for flat glass, but is not recommended for leaded glass or laminated glass.

Leaded glass panels should be individually wrapped in sheets of 1/4- to 1/2-inch-thick foam rubber batts and then tied with string or tape. Several of the wrapped panels are then stood on edge and tied snugly together. From this point on, the panels should always ride on edge and should never be laid flat. The crate for the panels should allow for 3 or 4 additional inches of space on all sides—top and bottom, as well as both ends. This space should be filled with some lightweight packing material, such as Styrofoam pellets, sufficiently compacted into place so that there is little chance of the panels shifting about in transit. The crate should be sufficiently strong, so that the sides cannot be staved in by accident. In addition to labeling the crate "Glass-Fragile," it should also be plainly marked "Ride On Edge-Never Lay Flat." Before making the crate, consider the weight of the panels it will carry; a very heavy crate is more susceptible to damage than a light one, simply because it is more awkward to handle. Thus, it is a better idea to use several crates, if necessary, to keep the weight proportion within safe boundaries. Leaded glass weighs about 4 pounds per square foot.

Naturally, stained glass work should never be shipped without sufficient insurance coverage. In case of damage, you must be prepared to substantiate your claim with some definite proof of value, such as invoices, letters of agreement, or similar papers.

It is good practice to enclose a note in the crate about how to handle the panels until they can be installed. They should be stored on edge, for example, and not laid flat. If possible, the crate should be unpacked in the presence of the deliverer, so that any damage can be verified. If the crate arrived in damaged condition or suspicious rattles are heard before the crate has been opened, a representative of the carriers should be called, and the crate should be opened in his presence.

Faceted slab glass panels are much less fragile than leaded panels, but, because of their greater weight (approximately 10 pounds per square foot), need a different kind of packing. A convenient method is to notch some lumber (such as "2 by 4s") so that they will accommodate several of the panels set on edge. The bottom and sides of the crate are made first; the panels are then set, one at a time into place, with the top crosspieces of notched wood put on last and nailed into place. The space between the panels—about 2 inches—can be filled in with crumpled newspaper.

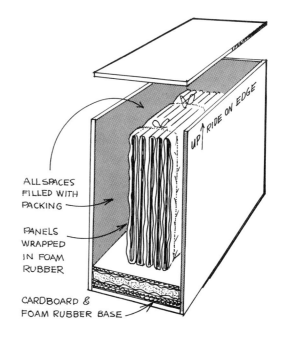

6-8. Stained glass panels should always "ride on edge." Wrapped panels are held upright, while packing material is placed into all spaces around and on top of panels.

It the entire crate doesn't have to be lifted, it can be made large enough to accommodate any number of panels. For example, the crate can be put into a truck and the panels put individually into the crate. When they reach their destination they are then unpacked from the same crate without its being lifted from the truck. If more than one carrier is involved, the entire shipment should be broken up into a number of crates so that the weight factor does not preclude their being easily handled.

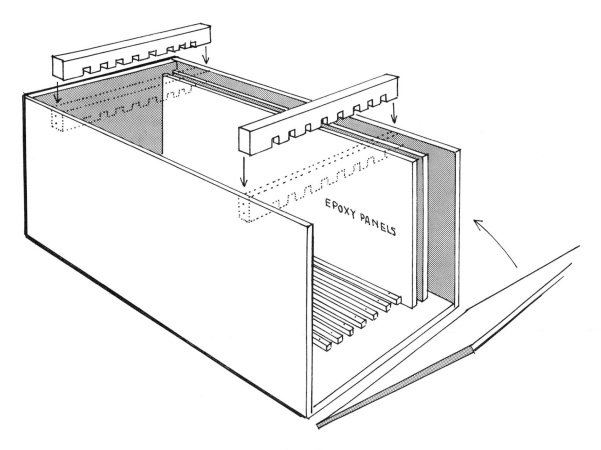

6-9. Schematic drawing showing method of crating faceted glass panels for shipment. All space around panels, including top and both ends of crate, can be stuffed with crumpled newspaper or similar packing.

CHAPTER 7.

STARTING YOUR OWN STUDIO

Some wit once observed that people working in the arts seemed to be more successful at "making a life" than they are at making a living. Maybe so; generally, the artist-craftsman has had neither the opportunity (or the inclination) to study "business methods" while preparing for his profession. Yet, he often practices his art in a world that takes such methods for granted. Also, it is in the nature of the artist's calling that it tends to be, more often than not, a solitary occupation. This makes for a kind of independence that should be highly prized by the artist (if it isn't simply taken for granted). But, like most things of value, it is not without its price. Most people in the visual arts (if not in the performing arts) generally operate without benefit of such things as collective bargaining, fixed wages, or fringe benefits, not to mention traditional professional guidelines so built-in to most other professions.

This is, perhaps, less true for the stained glass field than for most other branches of the arts, because it has historically been "craft-oriented." The state of the art, however, is rapidly changing; for one thing, vital new directions have unquestionably pushed some stained glass work into the realm of avant-garde art. In addition, a flowering of very imaginative work has invaded an area once dominated by an ancient tradition of methodology wedded to an often archaic liturgical symbolism. No longer is the question "Is it art or is it craft?" even valid; stained glass can now squarely confront the equation that measures all art—"skill in the service of imagination."

In our time, artistic people are regarded by society with somewhat ambivalent feelings; it is a mixture partly of admiration, partly of envy, and partly of suspicion. To those at that challenging stage of "branching out on their own," all of these are factors that bear thinking about. Are there any guidelines?

There seem to be three broad categories of stained glass activity today. The most recent is rather "gallery-oriented"; that is, it is concerned with the creation of highly personal, "autonomous" statements in glass. To suggest guidelines for the relatively few artists in this emerging realm would be a somewhat futile task, for the gallery "scene" has its own rather occult rules of the game.

At the other extreme are those stained glass artisans in pursuit of money through the mass production and sale of pseudo "period pieces" and stereotyped artifacts. They will sink or swim (perhaps in their own private pools?) according to the age old rules of the marketplace and its prevailing taste. To them we can only quote Ben Franklin: "Keep thy shop, and thy shop will keep thee," and wish them good-bye and good luck.

A third category is comprised of a growing number of stained glass artists who are allied with the art of architecture—be it in civil, commercial, or ecclesiastical buildings. Here, the architect enters the picture; for many commissions for contemporary work in stained glass, as well as for sculpture or murals, will come to you through the architect.

THE ARTIST AND THE ARCHITECT

If you get a commission from an architect for work, you will find that you may, in fact, be dealing with two parties—the architect and his client (which may sometimes consist of a building committee or a similar group).

Exploratory conversations with the architect should involve certain basic considerations—the kind of work you have done, (as shown by photographs of your work or a visit to your studio), total costs, sketches or models, time schedules, and so forth. As soon as something of a definite nature has been determined from these initial meetings, it is advisable for you, without too much delay, to sum it all up in the form of a confirming letter to the parties concerned, outlining everything in detail as complete as possible. In most cases, this letter will serve as a "letter of agreement." In fact, there is no reason why you should not label it so. Unless the architect or his client (or you) want something a little more elaborate in the way of a document in the legal sense, a letter of agreement forms a perfectly adequate basis for proceeding with the project. You should request that your letter of agreement be accepted and confirmed in writing by the other parties. In the event that some other form of agreement or contract is required by the architect or his client, it is then their responsibility to prepare the necessary papers for your signature. As standard operating procedure, it is good practice to keep a copy of every scrap of paper concerning the project, including letters, memos, costs, changes, and so forth, in a file.

If you make your agreement directly with the architect's client, rather than with the architect, there is a certain advantage. Should anything go wrong with the commission and you are forced into a legal hassle, you will be dealing directly with the ultimately responsible party (in the financial sense), rather than with his intermediary agent—the architect. In addition, your relationship with the architect is more apt to remain a harmonious one after the affair has been settled.

If this advice seems to be carrying caution to an extreme, it is offered with the observation that artists, as a group, are notoriously underfinanced. Their careers are particularly vulnerable should a setback occur.

THE ARTIST AS CONTRACTOR

Many architectural building projects involve a general or prime contractor who is responsible for the work performed by a variety of subcontractors (such as plumbing, electrical, masonry, and so forth). As the coordinator of work, the general contractor, under the architect's direction, sets schedules, checks on work in progress, and approves subcontractors' bills for work completed to be paid by the owner.

If you have been asked to do artwork in an architectural building project, you will inevitably have some dealings with the general contractor. Generally, your contract will be directly with the owners or architects, but sometimes they may prefer that your work be handled as a subcontract and channeled through the general contractor. Either way, however, you will be involved with the general contractor in terms of coordinating all the minor, but essential, questions that may come up. (But any questions relating to the quality of the design or the aesthetics of the situation, however, should be entirely between you and the owners or architect).

What are some of the items on which you will have to confer with the general contractor? As an example, if you are to do some stained glass windows for a building under construction, you must know not only the exact measurements of the openings as well as the details of the framing that has been specified, but you should also know the dates for "closing in" of the building (as distinct from the *completion date* of the project). Also, you should know whether additional work, such as plastering or painting, will be going on after the windows have been installed, for which the general contractor must take some precautions to assure that your work is not damaged. If you will need scaffolding for installing the work, it must be planned for in advance so that it will not intefere with other work scheduled.

To take another example, suppose you are to do artwork other than stained glass, say, a large sculpture. The general contractor should be informed at an early date if you plan to use heavy equipment for installing the finished piece; whether you will have a crew of helpers, the details on the hardware or "engineering" of the installation — and such questions of a similar nature.

There is yet another category of artwork in architecture in which you may be hired directly by a subcontractor (such as the interior designer or the landscape architect). You then become, in effect, a sub-subcontractor and you may have no dealings with either the owners or project architect.

In any event, it is always good practice to clear your plans with the management level of the general contractor, then get in touch with the field foreman of the project and apprise him of what is planned. The cooperation of the foreman can be very helpful to the smooth course of your project.

From the foregoing, it is pretty evident that if you get involved with artwork for architecture, you must find the best means of fitting into the tempo and special demands of that particular world. Because of the nature of his creativity, the artist/craftsman should not be pigeon-holed, as it were, under some heading of the building trades. Good construction skills, such as carpentry, concrete work, bricklaying, etcetera, do require extensive training and experience to achieve a high level of craftsmanship. This is also true for the artist; but an important distinction is that the artist is valued for his imagination, his ability to improvise and visualize — rather than to perform to a standard, established routine.

For the artist to take a lofty attitude about this, however, would be simply unrealistic, and probably something of a hindrance to his work. In fact, he had better be prepared to face the fact that a surprising number of people, including some architects, tend to categorize the artist working in architecture as being a kind of journeyman crafter, able to turn out art by the yard and on pretty short notice. Those who are at the stage of trying to establish their own studio — as well as their reputation — must have the psychological resilience to deal with such facts of life, and — in turn — to wage their own educational campaign whenever the opportunity presents itself.

WARM CREATIVITY AND COLD ECONOMICS
How much should you charge for a work of art? This is one of those questions you must face for which there is really no precise answer; yet, you are expected to come up with exactly that. Obviously, you must charge "enough" or you'll eventually find yourself in another field of endeavor, quite unrelated to the art of cost accounting.

To begin with, ask what kind of budget the architect or client may have set aside for art work in the building program. If none has been established, you should then ask what the finances might *allow* to be spent on the work. If the answers to these questions are still negative or somewhat vague, it will then be up to you to come up with an estimate *after* you have been able to study the situation fully. But you should hesitate, of course, to put much time into sketches or estimates until you have at least some rough idea of what's financially feasible and what is not.

There are several approaches to coming up with an estimate. Try to decide how much time you will need to complete the work from start to finish. Multiply this by the hourly or daily scale of wages you feel your ability and experience should command. Add to this your fixed overhead expenses (rent, utilities, equipment, the cost of maintaining your working space for the portion of time you will spend on the work, and so forth.) Add the cost of materials and additional labor or hired services you will need. The sum of this will be your bid, or the financial part of your proposal. In short, the equation runs like this: *time* multiplied by *wages* plus *fixed overhead* plus *materials/labor/services costs* equals bid. (Your *profit* in the above is really represented by *wages*.)

An alternative method is to charge on a "flat fee plus costs" basis. In this case, you must first estimate total *costs* (overhead, materials, special tools, and labor and services to be contracted plus any other similar expenses). To this is added your fee. Your fee remains fixed; the costs, which you must be prepared to substantiate, can vary more or less within reasonable bounds.

An important item that may be either built-in or added on to your bid, or proposal, is the stipulation of a sum for delivery charges, if necessary. You should consider, too, the possible risks to the art work during the transportation, whether this will be done by you, the client, or a freight carrier; you may want the protection of some additional, special insurance. If your client picks up the work from your studio, your responsibility ends there, provided that this factor has been written into the agreement.

Changes that you may be asked to make or changes that you have to make because of revisions (or errors) in building plans, could very well cost you additional expenses that must then be added on to your total costs. It is the architect's responsibility to supply you with a "change-order," which will justify any additional costs; however, you had better make it your business to request that the change-order be issued to you during, not after, the completion of the project.

Part of your proposal should include a stipulation as to *when* you will be paid. It is not a good idea to wait until after the project is completed to send in your total bill. Obviously, you will need some operating capital while the work is in progress. A convenient plan that answers this need is to specify receipt of one-third the total cost as down payment upon agreement to proceed, one-third when half the project is completed, and the final third upon completion and acceptance of the commission. If the project is a long-term affair, however, you should ask for an arrangement of scheduled monthly payments.

It also seems reasonable, if not mandatory, to try to acquaint yourself with the going rates that are being charged for similar art work in stained glass, murals, or sculpture; not so much for its value as a "fixed" scale, but rather as some indication to you that you are neither pricing yourself out of the market nor going broke on the installment plan.

The solution often comes down to that cold-blooded basis of "cost per square foot," which the art of architecture has long dealt with as an everyday reality. Granted that this sort of art-to-money ratio has only a peripheral relationship to aesthetics; nevertheless, it can vitally influence your survival as a creative person. I like Henri Matisse's statement to the effect that "art has nothing to do with money; therefore, let us get the best prices we can for our paintings."

There is a line beyond which art stops and something else begins. For example, an artist should avoid, whenever possible, becoming involved directly with the installation of his work. In the area of stained glass work, this is best left to a commercial glass contractor; they have the special experience, the proper tools, the right sealant materials. (They also have risk insurance, a state contractor's license, bondability, unions, and so on.) Try to ensure that good communications flow between you and the installer about all details concerned.

SKETCHES

You should have a strict rule that sketches or models will be charged-for, and this fact should be brought out early in the game. This way, if the project should have to be cancelled for some unpredicted reason or awarded to some other artist, you will at least be paid for the time you have invested in the sketches. You can, however, suggest that the sketch fee is applicable to the total cost of the *completed* commission.

Preliminary designs are an all-important first step because they frequently generate that spark of interest that gets a project off to a good start. If something unique in style, approach, or technique is going to be created, it is in the sketch that the idea begins to live and grow.

In a sketch, your idea must be visualized in its completed form and then be accepted by the architect or (Heaven help you) the committee. Architects, by the very nature of their training, are generally good visualizers, but their clients are frequently not. Thus, the ability to communicate what is sometimes of a germinal and ambiguous nature is an important facet of the versatility that the artist should possess. Something that the layman often doesn't appreciate is that the preliminary designs inevitably represent arduous creative work and can be time-consuming as well. In the final analysis, the sketch or model may be accepted or rejected, which is, of course, a client's right. But a point to note is that you have been asked to make sketches or models *after* having shown your client the general style and caliber of your work; thus, there is ample justification for your charging a sketch fee.

The foregoing comprises only the briefest introduction to some basic guidelines for those concerned with making a living in stained glass or any of the visual arts. There are several national organizations for artists and craftspeople that have published a variety of recommendations regarding such things as record keeping, taxes, galleries, copyrights, and other fun subjects. A description of these organizations is given in the Appendix.

APPENDIX

SUPPLIERS OF STAINED GLASS MATERIALS
Antique glass, coloured sheet glass, cast slab glass, streaky opalescent and streaky rolled cathedral glass.

Heatons paints and stains, copperfoil adhesive rolls, glass cutters, glass pliers, solder sticks and flux, U-came lead, electric soldering irons, lampshade kits ('Tiffany' type), jewels faceted for Tiffany lamps, hammers—tungsten tipped for breaking cast slabs.

James Hetley & Co. Ltd.,
Beresford Avenue,
Wembley, Middx.
01-903-4151

Lead cames

Heaps, Arnold & Heaps Ltd.,
Clarence Road,
Leeds, LS10 1UB.
0532-32519

Epoxy resin (Eccobond 24)
(It comes in 1 kilo or 4 kilo kits)

Emerson & Curning (UK) Ltd.,
1, South Park Road,
Scunthorpe,
South Humberside, DN17 2BY.
0724-63281

Electric kilns

R. M. Catterson-Smith,
Tollesbury,
Nr. Maldon,
Essex, CM9 8S5.
062-186-342

Brushes

From any supplier of artists' materials

Badger brushes

Hamilton & Co. Ltd.,
Rosslyn House,
Rosslyn Crescent,
Harrow, Middx.
01-427-1405

Leaded light cement

Peter Hodgson & Co.,
Wilbert Lane,
Beverley, Yorks.
Beverley 883221

MISCELLANEOUS SUPPLIES
C & R Loo German Imports
1550 62nd St.
Emeryville, Calif. 94662

Nervo Distributors
650 University Ave.
Berkeley, Calif. 94710

Whittemore-Durgin Glass
P.O. Box 2065
Hanover, Mass. 02339

SUPPLIER OF EPOXY GROUT FOR LAMINATED WINDOWS
Texas Refinery Corp.
P.O. Box 711
Ft. Worth, Tex. 76101

(specify: "Troxymite," fine grade)

PERIODICALS
Subscriptions are available to two authoritative periodicals, both of which feature a wide variety of articles on the world of stained glass. They also carry current information on supply sources from all parts of the country in their advertising columns. These periodicals are:
1. *Stained Glass,* a quarterly published by the Stained Glass Ass. of America, 1125 Wilmington Ave., St. Louis, Mo. 63111.
2. *Glass Art* published monthly. Write to 7830 S.W. 40th Ave., Portland, Oreg. 97219.

ART/CRAFT ORGANIZATIONS
The American Crafts Council is a nonprofit, educational organization with a national membership representing all of the crafts fields. It sponsors exhibits and forums and seeks to promote the status of the craft movement throughout the United States. The ACC publishes a bimonthly magazine called *Craft Horizons.* Subscribing members also receive *Outlook,* the Council's newsletter and are given free admission to the Museum of Contemporary Crafts. The address is: American Crafts Council, 44 W. 53rd St., New York, N.Y. 10019.

Artists Equity Association is a national, nonpolitical, aesthetically nonpartisan organization which represents the professional artists in America. AEA endeavors to promote and protect the interests of all professional visual artists; it works to promote legislation that will benefit the profession and to prevent or abolish abuses to the artist in his professional dealings with persons or organizations. Members receive an *AEA Newsletter* and other publications on such topics as copyright, income tax, art and architecture, inheritance tax, plus a calendar of current exhibits. There are local chapters from coast to coast. The address of the National Headquarters is: Artists Equity Ass., 3726 Albemarle Street, Washington, DC 20016.

The Guild for Religious Architecture represents the collaborative efforts of architects, clergymen, craftsmen, and artists to improve the aesthetic and functional design of religious buildings. An affiliate of the American Institute of Architects, the Guild is a nonprofit, educational organization. It publishes *Faith and Form* magazine, which is a review of information on problems of design and liturgy as they affect architecture and its allied arts. The Guild sponsors a religious-arts traveling exhibit, conferences, seminars and lectures, and maintains a color-slide library. Membership is open to architects, artists, and those interested in liturgical design. The address is: Guild for Religious Architecture, 1777 Church St. N.W., Washington, D.C. 20036.

The Stained Glass Association of America is a nonprofit organization founded in 1903 for the purpose of promoting the development of the stained glass craft. Membership is composed of stained glass studios, craft suppliers, stained glass artists, and associates, all working together to improve upon and advance the awareness, understanding, appreciation, and potentialities of the craft among all peoples. Members of the Association are located in many countries around the world, as well as in the United States. The SGAA maintains an apprenticeship program, holds annual conferences, and publishes the illustrated quarterly magazine called *Stained Glass.* The address is: Stained Glass Ass. of America, 1125 Wilmington, St. Louis, Mo. 63111.

The National Endowment for the Arts annually endows grants to artists/craftsmen and is a clearinghouse of information regarding government support of all the arts. There are branches in every state of the Union. The address is: National Endowment for the Arts, Washington, D.C. 20506.

BIBLIOGRAPHY

Duncan, Alastair. *Leaded Glass, A Handbook of Techniques.* New York: Watson-Guptill Publications, 1975.

Duval, Jean Jacques. *Working in Stained Glass.* New York: Thomas Y. Crowell Company, 1972.

Isenberg, Anita and Seymour. *How to Work in Stained Glass.* New York: Chilton Book Company, 1972.

Lee, Lawrence. *Stained Glass.* New York: Oxford University Press, 1967.

Metcalf, Gertrude and Robert, *Making Stained Glass.* New York: McGraw-Hill Book Company, 1972.

Mollica, Peter. *Stained Glass Primer.* Berkeley, Ca.: Mollica Stained Glass Press, 1971.

Reyntiens, Patrick. *Technique of Stained Glass.* New York: Watson-Guptill Publications, 1967.

INDEX